ĔMINENT

ESOTERIC PRAGUE

CHARLES BRIDGE

ESOTERIC PRAGUE

JAKUB MALINA

CHARLES BRIDGE

A Guide to the History and Esoteric Concept
of the Well-Known Masterpiece
of Charles IV and Peter Parler

CONTENTS

· III ·
THE BRIDGE
BETWEEN THE WORLDS

· IV ·
THE BRIDGE TO KNOWLEDGE

· V ·
EUROPEAN BRIDGES AND ART

To the Brothers of Golgotha

ISBN 978-80-7281-305-6

Both banks of the Vltava River, where the city of Prague is now situated, were settled much earlier than people and existing records can remember. It was perhaps the shallow water of the river with the old Celtic name Vltava that attracted people to settle near the river crossing, a threshold (práh in Czech) in the river, perhaps the magic of the place amidst the Czech basin, or perhaps both.

Over the centuries, small settlements on both riverbanks have grown into a large city that, thanks to its fortunate location, started turning into a magical place. The threshold connecting both riverbanks has changed with time, as has the city itself. The ordinary river crossing became first a wooden bridge, then a stone bridge; the regular threshold in the river became a threshold between worlds. And the nameless settlements turned into magical Prague.

We do not often really know why thousands of visitors are always so enchanted by this city. The magic seems to have been there since ever and is still seeping up from the old cobble stone pavement. We walk by such places, take delight in their beauty, are intoxicated by their magical power, and yet we do not see anything tangible.

Let's go to one of the places where the effects of mysterious Prague are the most powerful. Let's unveil how those of long-ago, who understood more than we do, used to work. If we listen carefully and forgive the author some of his clumsy words, we shall perhaps find a door leading to new knowledge.

The gate of esoteric Prague is open. All we have to do is enter.

Jakub Malina, 2007

· I ·

THE BRIDGE
OVER THE RIVER

JUDITH'S BRIDGE

The first bridge over the Vltava River near the Jewish settlement was made of wood. Although it is not by far the largest river in the world, it showed its power from time to time and destroyed the bridge which was being used by many people from near and far. One of the oldest reports on the destruction of the bridge is over a thousand years old and talks about how the wooden bridge was taken down by a flood in 929. After that, the bridge was destroyed many times. And water has been showing its power and proving the inability of people to be in charge of nature to this day.

The idea to join both banks of the Vltava River with a stone bridge is being attributed to Daniel, son of Zdislav of Lipé, who was elected the thirteenth bishop of Prague in 1148. He died of the plague during a crusade near Ancona on 9 August 1167. Only his bones, thoroughly boiled and free of flesh, returned to Bohemia.

After the wooden bridge was destroyed in the late 1150s, Bishop Daniel accompanied King Vladislav II[1] on a crusade in Italy where he became inspired by stone bridges. Back then stone bridges were practically unknown in Central Europe. The only two stone bridges north of Italy were in Würzburg (founded in 1133) and over the Danube River in Regensburg, called Ratisbon back then, through which both men often passed. The bridge over the Danube River had three towers and it took 470 steps to cross it.

---

[1] Vladislav II was the nineteenth historically proven Premyslid who ruled in Bohemia. In the year of 1147, he took part in the second crusade. Due to some problems, he did not reach Jerusalem, but visited for example Constantinople and the Kiev Russia. He ruled from 1140 to 1172. In the year of 1158, Vladislav II was crowned the second Czech king for helping Friedrich Barbarossa.

STONE-MASONS IN BOHEMIA

The bishop's idea found support at the royal court. In particular, Queen Judith from Thuringia, the second wife of Vladislav II, became a generous benefactress of the future bridge. An experienced Italian stone-mason, whom Daniel befriended in Italy and Prague inhabitants later on nicknamed Bradáč, was in charge of the construction.

Of course, Master Bradáč was not able to make such a grand project by himself. He needed many educated experts, whom, however, he could not find in Bohemia in spite of the good craftsmanship of the local people. Therefore, Bradáč brought them from all over the Holy Roman Empire and founded the first large stone-cutting works in Prague. This gave the Prague architecture a significant boost from abroad.

As we have already mentioned in our journey after the mysteries of the Prague Horologe, lay stone-cutting guilds were free societies of artisans, exempt from serfdom and having their own legislation, customs, and language. In addition to their knowledge of geometry, drawing, and architecture, they secretly engaged in hermetic sciences. They continued with the tradition of even more mysterious spiritual orders, such as the Cistercians and the Knights Templars, that had witnessed the onset of a revolutionary architectural style — the Gothic style — in France at the beginning of the 12th century.

Both these orders were already active in Prague. The Knights Templars came to Prague during the rule of Wenceslas I around 1230 and owned the

The first stone bridge in Prague was built just several meters south of one of today's busiest tourist places in the city. It ended on the Old Town bank, approximately where the buildings of the Order of Crusaders are now.

Monastery and Church of St. Lawrence, also called *In Jerusalem*, until 1313. The order was dissolved by the Bull of Vienna in 1312, i.e. five years after Western Europe started the horrid extermination of this order. The Order of Cistercians came to Prague in 1142. The Premonstratensians, who founded their Prague monastery in Strahov two years before the arrival of the Cistercians, also engaged in construction.

THE FIRST STONE BRIDGE

The stone bridge over the Vltava River was finished in 1172. According to the letter of Canon Vincentius of the Prague Church addressed to Judith, the bridge was built in just three years! And it was a very impressive bridge for that time indeed: it had twenty-eight bridge pillars and a paved bridge deck 514 meters long and 7 meters wide, its pillars were about half the size of the bridge vaults, it had new icebreakers and a huge stone curb, and it was built in a much deeper river than the one over the Danube River in Regensburg.

Yellow and red gritstone used for the bridge was quarried near Zápy by Brandýs. The deck was made of Drabov quartzite pointed with lime mortar. In order to lay the bridge foundations, cofferdams of wooden stakes were constructed, water was then pumped out of the inner cavity, using volute

There is not much left of the original Judith's Bridge. We can see only a small part of the original stone deck of the bridge in front of the so-called Grapevine Column at the corner of the Church of St. Francis at Crusaders Square. It is one of the oldest pavements in Prague.

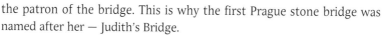

The portrayal of an unknown Italian stone master, who built Judith's Bridge, was moved to the navigation of Charles Bridge in the 19th century. The relief can be seen from the statue of St. Bernard on Charles Bridge. In its original place, Master Bradáč's relief also served as an indicator of the level of water. If his head is under water, it means that the city may be flooded.

pumps or treadwheels, and a clay--packed wooden grillage was placed on the bottom. Heavy blockstones for pillars were then put on top of the grillage.

After Daniel's death, Queen Judith, who financed the construction, became the patron of the bridge. This is why the first Prague stone bridge was named after her — Judith's Bridge.

As its wooden predecessors, Judith's Bridge had to face huge floods. Even though the stone bridge was much stronger than the wooden ones, its foundations were not always able to endure the enormous pressure of water and drifting ice and timber and it was often damaged. In 1252, a hospital of the Brotherhood of Crusaders was founded on the Old Town riverbank and, a year later, became the keeper of the bridge by the order of Wenceslas I. To pay for necessary repairs, the hospital brothers collected a bridge toll and used proceeds from the property donated by the king. When the bridge broke, they even organized alms across the entire Bohemia.

THE GOTHIC PROMISE

The new royal stone-cutting works were near the walls of the Monastery of the Virgin Mary by the river crossing over the Vltava River, which was just a few steps from the place that Bradáč chose for the new bridge. The arrival of Bradáč's stone-masons and journeymen in the 1160s and the development of spiritual construction orders paved the way for the transition from the Romanesque style to the Early Gothic style in Bohemia.

Yet many years had to pass by before the majestic Gothic style, charged with esoteric knowledge, made its firm roots in Bohemia. The first magnificent building in the Early Gothic style — the Convent of St. Agnes — was not built until sixty years after Judith's Bridge. And it took another four decades before the next sacral edifice in the Early Gothic style — the Old New Synagogue — was erected in the back-then Jewish ghetto in Prague.

Although Judith's Bridge is gone now, except for a few remains on the bottom and banks of the Vltava River, the face of its first builder has been on the bridge to this day. Bradáč's sculptured self-portrait was moved from the remains of Judith's Bridge to Charles Bridge in 1840 where, veiled with legends, it indicates the level of water in the Vltava River.

JUDITH'S TOWER

However, the relief of Bradáč, which is easy to see from the statue of St. Bernard on the second pillar, and the first bridge vault hidden under the Monastery of Crusaders are not the only remnants of the ancient Judith's Bridge. On the other side of the Vltava River, there is a Romanesque bridge tower, sometimes called Judith's Tower. When looking toward the Prague Castle, it is the lower tower on the left creating, with its higher Gothic counterpart, a gate ending the present Charles Bridge on the Lesser Town side.

The tower originally had three stories. In the past, it witnessed many armed conflicts and fights over this important bridge. The first information about the tower comes from August 1249. A year later, on 17 December 1250, Knight Pertolt, the oldest ancestor of the Bohdanecký dynasty of Hodkov, was crossing the bridge. Two ravens fighting on top of the tower knocked down a loose stone that fell on the knight's head and killed him. Supposedly, the stone was not put back for a long time.

When the followers of John of Luxembourg fought Henry of Carinthia, fire destroyed the third story of the tower, giving the tower its current look. The tower contains an important monument — one of the oldest Romanesque basreliefs in the Czech territory.

The rather damaged basrelief was discovered by accident in the 19th century and probably depicts the bridge builder receiving a model of the bridge or some other symbol from the king — builder.

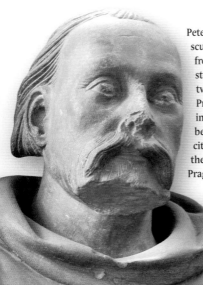

Peter Parler was an ingenious builder and talented sculptor of European caliber. He came to Prague from Schwäbisch Gmünd, where he worked in the stone-cutting works of his father, Henry. As a twenty-three-year-old young man, he was invited to Prague by Emperor Charles IV and asked to run the imperial stone-cutting works. In Bohemia, which became his new home, Peter Parler was a respected citizen of both Prague towns and was in charge of the construction of the Cathedral of St. Vitus at the Prague Castle, Charles Bridge, and many other religious and secular edifices. His work, full of mysterious symbols and signs, proves that he was an initiate of a high degree and was a part of the close circle of artists at the imperial court. He died on 13 July 1399 at the age of sixty-seven.

THE STONE BRIDGE

The same year, on the eve of the Purification of the Virgin Mary, after a warm southern wind that brought spring rain and after a very harsh winter during which many people in Bohemia and other countries froze to death, melting snow and heavy rain caused a huge flood. Drifting thick sheets of ice took down the Prague bridge in several places, sparing only about one-fourth of it, which, however, was also damaged by rushing water and drifting ice.

František Pražský: Kronika [Chronicle], middle of the 14th century

When, on the unfortunate 3 February 1342, another huge flood destroyed three-fourths of Judith's Bridge, chronicler František Pražský wrote: *"When the famed bridge came down, it was as if the crown of the kingdom fell…"* The pride of the city was gone forever. Both back-then existing Prague towns were separated again by the water of the Vltava River.

Even though the absence of a bridge connecting both Vltava banks very much complicated the transportation, Charles IV first founded the Prague University and had the largest construction project in Europe of the 14th century, the Prague New Town and its fortifications, built. Only then did the ruler have a completely new bridge built. ▷

It took fifteen and a half years before King Charles IV founded a new stone bridge replacing the old one. Even though in the 1330s and 1340s, Italian stone-masons were building a bridge in Roudnice, there were obviously not enough qualified people and money, which was being collected in the entire Bohemia, to rebuild the so much needed bridge in Prague. However, the long time of preparations that Charles IV put in was not a waste since he designed a project worthy of a ruler of his caliber. He tasked his court master builder, the young esoteric Peter Parler, who was also building the cathedral at the Prague Castle, with the construction of the bridge.

A GRANDIOUSE PROJECT

Always thinking about how to ameliorate the Czech Lands and the City, in which he was born, and about his legacy left to future generations, Emperor Charles ordered to build a high and very strong bridge across the Vltava River connecting the Lesser Town and the Bigger Town and he himself laid the first stone near the Monastery of St. Climent. On this bridge, he had a beautiful tower with very profond and strong stone foundations built across from the Royal Hospital. He wanted the Gate, under which people would pass, to be like no other gate in the Christian world and asked to hurry with the construction so that it would be finished during his lifetime.

Václav Hájek of Libočany, Kronika Česká [Czech Chronicle], 1818

The basic parameters of Peter Parler's bridge are indeed very impressive for that time. The bridge, made of sandstone blocks, is 515.76 meters long and 9.5 meters wide and rests on 16 vaults of uneven span ranking from 16.62 meters to 23.38 meters. The Prague bridge was one of the largest bridges of the 14th century.

Just for a comparison — the deck of Judith's Bridge used to be about 4 to 5 meters lower than that of the new bridge. Peter Parler hardly used any remains of the original bridge, creating a completely

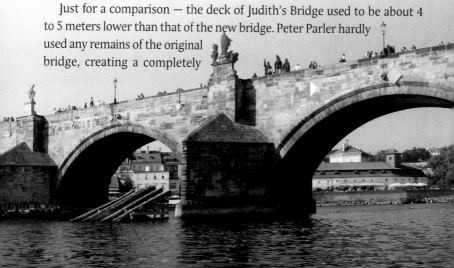

new bridge. The only thing that the Stone Bridge had in common with the old Judith's Bridge was the gate on the Lesser Town bank. The Old Town Bridge Tower was moved more to the south. The bridge does not cross the river in a straight line but in an almost exact eastwestern direction, and, when reaching the Kampa Island, it curves toward the Lesser Town Gate.

FLOODS ON THE VLTAVA RIVER

With such a size and magical protection, the Prague bridge was destined to last forever. However, the Vltava River was always very unpredictable, and thus even such a well-constructed bridge suffered some damage from time to time.

The Stone Bridge was struck by a flood for the first time in 1432 when water took down five pillars. However, the bridge was repaired and ready to provide transportation between the two Prague banks for the next several centuries. A flood in 1784 damaged the bridge quite a bit and so did the one that came a hundred years later, in 1890, taking down two pillars and three vaults. During these floods, not only parts of the

Darstellung der Grossen Überschwemmung und Eiß stosses vom 27 biß 28 Februarÿ 1784 in Prag.

bridge but also people, watch-houses, and statues decorating the bridge fell into the water.

Charles Bridge, closely watched by people in live television broadcasting, survived the last huge flood that Prague witnessed in the summer of 2002. After several days of holding up against raging water, the bridge came out of it practically undamaged, losing not even one stone or statue.

A HISTORICAL NOTE

Since its foundation in the 14th century, Charles Bridge has seen history go by. The bridge has witnessed many more or less important events and survived several military attacks that could have totally destroyed it.

In the year of 1420, the Hussites crossed the bridge to get to the Lessor Town. It is believed that they damaged the cross mounted onto one of the pillars. In the year of 1648 at the end of the Thirty-Year War, Charles Bridge was the place of a merciless battle between the army of the Swedish conqueror Königsmark, who occupied the hill with the Prague Castle and the Lessor Town bank, and Old Town burgesses. The bridge suffered a lot of damage. At last, peace, putting a stop to the war so trauma-

A tramway with a special bottom power feed system used to run on the bridge until the year of 1908.

tizing for Bohemia, was negotiated right on the bridge. Fighting during the uprising of 1848 also damaged the bridge and its surroundings.

Throughout the centuries, Charles Bridge saw many prominent rulers — solemn coronation processions of Czech kings and queens and the panic flee of the Czech Winter King Frederick of Palatinate after the lost Battle of White Mountain on 8 November 1620 — as well as many renowned scientists and artists. Charles Bridge inspired Jaroslav Seifert, a Czech poet and winner of the Nobel Prize in literature, to write a collection of poems.

Oil lighting on the bridge was introduced in 1723. In the year of 1785, the bridge was connected to the island, called Kampa since 1770, with a stairway that was reconstructed and widened in 1844. On 1 August 1883, a tramway pulled by horses provided transportation across the bridge; in the year of 1905, this tramway was replaced by an electric one. In order not to spoil the look of the bridge and not to interfere with the view of the

The oldest portrayal of Charles Bridge is probably that on the painting by Jan van Eyck, The Virgin of Chancellor Rolin, from 1435.

Prague Castle and statues on the bridge, the 770-meter-long tramway rails had a special bottom power feed system made by František Křižík. However, the tramway ran only for three years.

The last major repair of the historical bridge was carried out between 1965 and 1974. During that time, it was decided to stop the automobile traffic on Charles Bridge and to make the bridge a pedestrian zone. However, it seems that with the growing tourism in Prague, the bridge will soon be too small for pedestrians as well.

THE OLD TOWN BRIDGE TOWER

The Old Town Bridge Tower is surely one of the most beautiful Gothic edifices in Europe. And as such, it has been always thoroughly studied by historians, artists, and mystics, and thus we can find different descriptions and interpretations of its rich stone adornment in many books and publications on Prague and Charles Bridge. Let's summarize them and add some of our own little observations.

FOUNDATION OF THE TOWER

The tower situated on the first pillar of Charles Bridge has the shape of a two-story prism with spires and a high slate, tent-shaped roof. On the southern side, there is a prismal addition with its own roof and stairway connecting the floors of the tower.

The tower was built by the stone-cutting works of Peter Parler in 1357. The monumental vault of the passage was not finished until 1373, and the entire tower was most likely completed around 1380.

The sculptural adornment on the eastern side of the tower, most likely created by Peter Parler himself, has remained practically intact to this day. The original sculptural adornment on the western part of the tower was destroyed during the fights with the Swedish army in 1648.

The two-story Old Town Bridge Tower with its Gothic adornment belongs among the most admired monuments in Europe. The tower with its adornment is the masterpiece of Parler's stone-cutting works.

The vault of the tower passage is without any doubt one of the most remarkable architectonical works of Peter Parler. The system of opposite, interconnected, and inversely interlain patterns, the ribs of which come straight out of the walls without consoles and cross at springings, surpasses even the vault of the St. Wenceslas presbytery. Instead of a classical apex stone, the ingenious master builder placed a golden crown.

A BLOODY HISTORY

In the past, the Old Town Bridge Tower was not decorated only with Gothic sculptures of the so-called beautiful style. It witnessed some horrible things, in particular after the defeat of the Czech estates at the White Mountain on unfortunate gloomy Sunday, 8 November 1620; it is rather symbolic that the White Mountain is right behind the horizon to which the central line of Charles Bridge points.

Ferdinand II ruthlessly avenged himself for being humiliated by Czech noblemen who chose Frederick of Palatinate, known as the Winter King in Bohemia, as the Czech king. In May 1621, the Prague execution commission passed fifty-one death sentences. Twenty-seven of them were actually carried

The passage vault of the tower is one of the best works of the Late Gothic in Europe. The original painting was restored by the painter Petr Maixner in 1878.

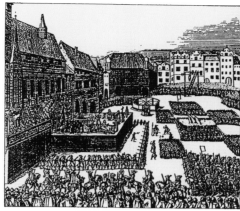

An engraving of the execution at the Old Town Square. On the left, Count Šlik is being beheaded.

out at the Old Town Square on 21 June 1621. Seventeen prominent burgesses, seven knights, and three noblemen were executed.

Executioner Mydlář had to display the heads of twelve executed men, among which was also President of Charles University Johann Jesenius, as a warning on the Old Town Bridge Tower. He placed their heads in metal baskets on long metal poles and hung them from the tower gallery. Six heads were shown on the eastern side and the other six on the western side. The rebels were to be publicly mocked by people. The executioner placed cut-off limbs on the heads of some of the rebels and the tongue, cut out alive, on the head of the university president.

According to historical records, after a storm on 11 March 1622, the basket with the head of Prokop Dvořecký of Olbramovice fell on the bridge and shortly after another head as well. However, at the emperor's order both heads had to be put back on the gallery of the tower. On 9 May 1622, the head of the most prominent executed man, Jáchym Ondřej Šlik, was taken off since the emperor decided to grant the wish of Countess Šlik and to take down the head of her executed husband so that she could bury it with the body. The remaining eleven heads kept decorating the gallery until the Saxon invasion of Prague in November 1631.

The remains of the executed men were then taken off the tower and reverently buried in the Tyn Church. When the Saxons were forced to leave Prague six months later, the chest with the remains was mysteriously lost and nobody has ever found it. Some legends say that it is still in a secret place in the Tyn Church, while others mention the Church of the Holy Savior.

Are the heads of the executed men that were taken off the Old Town Bridge Tower in 1631 still in the Tyn Church?

The rather famous bloody story with the heads of the executed Czech noblemen on the Old Town Bridge Tower was only a repetition of what had happened a century before. In the year of 1517, the cut-off head of another condemned nobleman was displayed on the opposite Lesser Town Bridge Tower. The executed person was Jindřich of Bohnice called Bohnička. He was a knight-bandit who attacked and looted the manors of Prague burgesses, and thus the city of Prague sent a group of men to capture him. They caught him in a pub by Jičín, injuring him gravely during a fight. Knight Bohnička did not survive the transportation to Prague. Still, the Prague people had him beheaded and his head displayed on the Lesser Town Bridge Tower. It could have been this cruelty of the Prague people that Ferdinand copied in his hideous act on the Old Town Bridge Tower a hundred years later.

RECONSTRUCTION OF THE TOWER

The Old Town Bridge Tower was damaged several times in the past. The first time it was in 1420, just forty years after its completion, when the Hussites passed through there on their way to the Lessor Town. During the Thirty--Year War, when Swedish soldiers were plundering the Prague Castle, the tower lost a large part of its adornment on the western side. Based on the documents of that time, we are able to reconstruct only the basic look and meaning of the adornment.

The municipal council had the remains of the destroyed adornment on the western façade of the Old Town Bridge Tower removed in 1779 so that they would not fall on people walking below. In the year of 1650, this façade was repaired by Carlo Lurago, a prominent master builder of the Prague Baroque, and stone-mason Giovanni Baptista Spinetti. At that time, a tablet with the city emblem, showing an arm holding a sword which was added on a year before by Emperor Ferdinand III, and with the following golden inscription commemorating the heroic fight of the Prague people defending the Old Town against the Swedish army was mounted onto the façade:

Siste hic paulisper viator sed lubens ac volens ubi multa populatus tandem vel invitus sistere debuit Gothoroum et Vandalorum furor et lege sculptum in marmore quod ad perpetuum Boemorum omnium sed inprimis vetero Pragensium memoriam anno Domini MDCXLVIII Mars suecicus ferro et igne in hac turri delineavit. Haec turris gothici fuit ultima meta furoris sed fidei non est haec ultima meta Boemiae. Voluissent id

ipsum Cives Vetero Pragenses fuso sanguine inscribere nisi pax aurea Ferdinandi III. pietate et justitia in orbem germanicum reducta pro sanguine aurum suppeditasset.

Ye who wander, stop gladly and willingly for a moment at this place where the plundering furor of the Goths and Vandals was put to a stop and read what the Swedish Mars has carved in marble with fire and sword on this tower in 1648 A.D. for the eternal glory of all Czechs, but above all Old Town citizens. The tower was the final target of the Goths' plundering, but it is not the final target of Czech loyalty. Old Town citizens would have written the same with their own blood if peace, brought back to the German Empire by the love and justice of Ferdinand III, had not offered gold instead of blood.

In order to repair the damage caused to city fortifications by the Swedish army, the Old Town received 300 thousand Rheinland guldens. The petition submitted prior to the payment states: *"Damage caused by shooting — 3000 fl."* What a low price demanded for the destruction of such a unique Gothic sculptural adornment. The entire bridge was then repaired for less than five thousand guldens.

The tower was also damaged during the uprising of 1848 and had to undergo a large reconstruction between 1874 and 1878, in charge of which was famous Czech restorer Josef Mocker.

Senior construction counselor Mocker (1835—1899), an architect, master builder, and restorer, was a typical representative of pseudo-Gothic purism of the second half of the 19th century. He studied at the Technical University and Academy of Visual Arts in Vienna. He became a member of the Czech Academy of Science and Art, designed new buildings, and participated in many completions and renovations of prominent churches and castles. In the year of 1873, he was asked to finish the Cathedral of St. Vitus at the Prague Castle and participated in the completion of the Cathedral of St. Stephan in Vienna, the renovation of the castle Karlstein, the castle Konopiště, the castle Křivoklát, the Powder Gate, and cathedrals in Kolín, Vysoké Mýto, and Pilsen.

His contemporaries often criticized his restoration work for deviating from the original nature of restored buildings. However, in respect to the reconstruction of the Old Town Bridge Tower, today's experts rather emphasize the deep respect that he showed when working on the tower. Based on his experience, Josef Mocker wrote several publications on restoring historical monuments. It was Mocker who gave the tower roof the shape as we know it today. During the years of 1877—1878, the painter Petr Maixner restored and finished the original Gothic painting in the tower passage.

· II ·

THE BRIDGE BETWEEN BANKS

Shame on you, the inconquerable king of the Quirites,
for using wood piles instead of marble to join the banks of the Tiber!
Look at the miraculous bridge over the Vltava River,
with its splendid light vaults creating a dam for waves
and statues from Synnadian marble made by the Phrygians,
standing proud since they were chiseled out by Mentor.

Quirin Mickl, abbot of the Cistercian Monastery in Vyšší Brod,
Praga Caput Regni, 18th century

THE TRIUMPHAL ARCH

The gate to Charles Bridge is an important part of the Royal Route, the old coronation route of Czech kings improved by Charles IV. The route started at Vyšehrad and ended at the Prague Castle. It is thus obvious that one of its functions was to present and celebrate the king. Historian Rudolf Chadraba noticed this triumphal symbology and provided a very detailed art historical interpretation of it.

CONSTANTINE'S INSPIRATION

The tower, which according to its founder Charles IV was to be one of a kind in the world, was modeled after the triumphal arches of Roman emperors. Just as the first Christian emperor Constantine, whom Charles admired, had bridges built across the Rhein River and the Danube River and especially had the Roman Bridge built in his royal seat of Trier, Charles IV had a stone bridge built in his royal seat that was to symbolically become the New Jerusalem and Renovated Rome, the holiest place of Christianity.

And just as the Constantine coronation route in Rome had traversed the Milvian Bridge over the Tiber River on which Constantine won a battle in 312, a thousand years later the Charles coronation route traversed the Stone bridge over the Vltava River. Emperor Constantine was still using the title *caesar pontifex maximus,* which means both caesar — high priest and caesar — bridge builder.

Raised in a religious spirit and educated in France, Charles must have considered himself the priest ascended to the Roman throne, of which his adversaries and disreputable interpreters of his work were quite aware. Vilém of Occam even

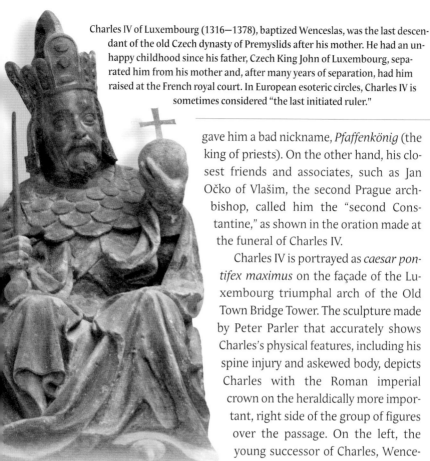

Charles IV of Luxembourg (1316—1378), baptized Wenceslas, was the last descendant of the old Czech dynasty of Premyslids after his mother. He had an unhappy childhood since his father, Czech King John of Luxembourg, separated him from his mother and, after many years of separation, had him raised at the French royal court. In European esoteric circles, Charles IV is sometimes considered "the last initiated ruler."

gave him a bad nickname, *Pfaffenkönig* (the king of priests). On the other hand, his closest friends and associates, such as Jan Očko of Vlašim, the second Prague archbishop, called him the "second Constantine," as shown in the oration made at the funeral of Charles IV.

Charles IV is portrayed as *caesar pontifex maximus* on the façade of the Luxembourg triumphal arch of the Old Town Bridge Tower. The sculpture made by Peter Parler that accurately shows Charles's physical features, including his spine injury and askewed body, depicts Charles with the Roman imperial crown on the heraldically more important, right side of the group of figures over the passage. On the left, the young successor of Charles, Wenceslas IV, with the Roman royal crown is portrayed as the second *caesar pontifex maximus*. Between them, standing on a bridge symbol, the old emblem of *fratres pontifices* (brothers — bridge builders), there is St. Vitus in the pose of the Roman god Apollo and with the face of Václav (Wenceslas) of Radeč, a canon of the Church of St. Apollinaris. He really resembles the bust of the canon made by Peter Parler in the St. Vitus triforium. The Apollo-style portrayal of the Christian martyr from Sicily is also emphasized by the relief of Daphne hidden in the adornment of the console under the saint's feet.

◁ The inspiration from the famous Roman emperor Constantine can be seen on the fresco above the door of the private chapel of Charles IV, the Chapel of St. Catherine, at the castle Karlstein. The Luxembourg emperor had himself portrayed from the profile, just as Constantine and his mother Helen did. As an initiate, he probably knew that the profile could say a lot about his fate — karma — to other esoterics.

The role of the portal of the Old Town Bridge Tower as a traditional imperial triumphal arch is also indicated by the round, non-Gothic arch above the heads of the Luxembourg rulers.

ROMAN FEMALE EAGLE AND CZECH LION

der louw bedütit Bëmer lant
der ar zü Röme milde fant

The lion representing the Czech Lands
found the love of the female eagle in Rome

Heinrich von Mügeln, 1350

The symbols of the Holy Roman Empire and the Czech Kingdom under festive carousel helmets, the ceremonial meaning of which we can find in ancient Persian symbology, heraldically bow down to the bridge with St. Vitus. The realistic relief of the non-heraldic lion, looking down with obvious endearment at the fiery St. Wenceslas female eagle on the emblem located above St. Vitus, refers to the ancient Czech prophecy from the time of Premysl Ottokar II. The prophecy of Abbot Joachim about the Last Ruler of Bohemia, who will conquer Rome, subjugate the pope, conquer Jerusalem (where he will then die), and convert pagans to Christianity, is also evoked in the poem by Heinrich von Mülgen from Charles IV's court.

The amorous play between the Czech lion and the female eagle symbolizing Rome culminates each year on the summer solstice, when the shadow of the lion touches the emblem with the female eagle for a very short moment at high noon only one day in a year. This symbolic play of an ephemeral moment refers to the Leonine couplet from Roman gates that as a palindrome — a magical trap that can be read from the right to the left and vice versa — is believed to be inscribed on the western side of the tower right under the roof:

Signa te, signa, temere me tangis et agnis
Roma, tibi subito motibus ibit amor
Cross thyself. You plague and vex me without
need. For by my efforts you are about to reach
Rome, the object of your travel.

The solstice mystery, during which the shadow of the statue of the lion touches the emblem with the female eagle just for a very short moment, is very famous. Unfortunately, this mystery is currently being hindered by safety nets around the sculptures on the Bridge (below left).

THE CULT OF VICTORY

Roman triumphal arches and columns always symbolized the cult of victory. Rudolf Chadraba explains that the Old Town Bridge Tower was also constructed as a triumphal arch. In addition to the already mentioned pose of St. Vitus as the *Victorious Apollo*, holding an olive branch that brings peace to the city, the other figures on the eastern façade are also charged with the symbology of victory.

The saint's name itself — Vitus — is etymologically connected with victory and saluting victors. His model, the ancient Slavic god Svantovít (Svantvitus), the cult of which St. Vitus replaced in Bohemia, was also called the Almighty Victor. The Christian name of Charles IV was Wenceslas, which is the name that Charles IV also gave to his son. This name in Latin transcription is *Venceslaus*, which comes from *vincens laus* in Latin meaning a laudation for the triumphant. The third person in the central group of statues, Václav

The face of the statue of St. Vitus resembles the fifth director of the construction of the Cathedral of St. Vitus, Václav of Radeč who, together with Charles IV baptized Wenceslas, Wenceslas IV, and St. Wenceslas on the column right in front of the gate, used to form a remarkable secret group of four Wenceslases.

(Wenceslas) of Radeč, has the same victorious name. The fourth Wenceslas in the group, St. Wenceslas, the patron of the Czech nation, used to be on a nearby column as we will talk about later on.

The names of both Czech patrons, Sigismund and Adalbert, bear similar signs of victory. While the German name Sigismund (*Sieges-mund*) of the Burgundian king can be best translated into Czech as *Vítězslav* (Victor), the Slavnik bishop St. Adalbert (Vojtěch) can be interpreted as the consolation of an army (*útěcha voje*). This is why the second son of the great emperor was called Sigismund.

The crown replacing the apex stone in the vault of the tower passage refers to the name of *St. Corona* whose bone Charles received, together with a relic of *St. Victor*, in Milan on the way to his Roman coronation. Charles IV collected their relics during his entire life and had a great respect for them.

The imperial orb, the symbol of eternal world supremacy of the Roman Empire, used to be adorned during the pagan times with the statue of the goddess of victory, the winged *Victoria*, on the globe. After Constantine's vision of a burning cross in the sky and the inscription of *in hoc signo vinces (in this sign you shall conquer)* just before the crucial battle of Milvian, he replaced the victorious Victoria with a victorious cross. This is why Roman Emperor Charles IV, Roman King Wenceslas IV, victorious Roman patron Sigismund, and the highest Christian patron of the Empire, St. Vitus, are holding an orb with a cross.

The statues of St. Adalbert and St. Sigismund belonged among the most prominent artworks at the representative exhibition of Gothic art from the era of the last Luxembourgs in New York and Prague in 2005 and 2006. Even though at the exhibition, Charles IV — Emperor by the Grace of God, and in the official exhibition catalog, the first statue presented as the statue of St. Prokop is definitely the Czech patron, the former Prague Bishop, St. Adalbert, based on the attributes. The original statues from the façade of the Old Town Bridge Tower can be seen in the Lapidarium of the National Museum at Výstaviště, Prague.

THE TRIUMPHAL COLUMN

Not too many people know that right in front of the Old Town Bridge Tower, in the center line of the gate, there used to be another symbol of victory — a triumphal column similar to Trajan's Column in Rome — with a statue of St. Wenceslas on the top. We do not know what the original Gothic statue of St. Wenceslas looked like, we can only guess based on the statue of this most prominent patron of the Czech nation made by Peter Parler and located in the Chapel of St. Wenceslas in the Cathedral of St. Vitus.

The column with the Baroque replacement of the statue of St. Wenceslas made by Jan Jiří Bendl was moved several times; first, to the corner of today's non-existing customs-house at Crusaders Square, then somewhere else. Today we can see it on the corner wall of the Church of St. Francis at

Crusaders Street. It is called the Grapevine Column or Wine-growing Column perhaps because its pedestal is entwined with stone grapevines and because St. Wenceslas is the patron of winegrowers. It is a known fact that he lived almost like a monk and made his own bread and wine to receive communion.

It is the triumphal column taking the dominant place in front of the triumphal gate, the special position of the St. Wenceslas female eagle on the eastern façade of the gate, the St. Wenceslas crown at the top of the vault, and the face of four different Wenceslases in the principal figural motif of the façade that make us somewhat doubt the common belief that the bridge, similarly to the Cathedral of St. Vitus, was dedicated to St. Vitus whose sculpture is on the tower. The frequency and prominent position of the Wenceslas adornment rather indicate a dedication to St. Wenceslas, which, however, the passage of time has effaced. It is possible that, similarly to the cathedral, the bridge was dedicated to both saints; the protector of the empire played a dominant role in the Cathedral of St. Vitus while the protector of the kingdom did on the bridge situated below the cathedral. St. Wenceslas protected the bridge and its towers, while St. Vitus welcomed victors and brought eternal peace to the city, *pax romana.*

The doubts about the dedication of the bridge are also supported by the St. Wenceslas legend itself. After Prince Wenceslas had been killed by the retinue of his brother in Stará Boleslav, his body was buried in the local church. When, three years later, the penitent fratricide Boleslav wanted to move the body to the first church of St. Vitus founded by Wenceslas at the Prague Castle, the retinue encountered unexpected problems. According to the legend, the transported saint had to actually help the retinue to get over the swollen

St. Wenceslas is considered the founder of the winegrowing tradition. Therefore, people call his statue, nowadays placed at the corner of Crusaders Square, the Grapevine Column. The symbology of the grapevine entwining a column may also refer to the old mysterious tradition of the staff, thyrsos. In esoteric tradition, Premyslid Prince Wenceslas is considered one of the last early medieval initiates of the Holy Grail.

Rokytka River. And that is not all; the Prague bridge, back then still the wooden one, appeared over the horizon shortly after...

Rushing toward the Vltava River and seeing that the bridge was broken, they began lamenting since they were also very exhausted. Unable to lift the saint's body, they commenced praying so that he would show his mercy again and spare their young lives since the morning cock-crowing, the hour set by the prince, had just started. And soon they understood that he had answered their prayers, they lifted him up on their shoulders as if he weighed nothing, and crossed the broken bridge, while giving their thanks to God.

Kristiánova legenda [Christian's Legend], end of the 10th century

Even though history and philology scholars have been debating since the 19th century whether Christian's Legend is from the 10th century or the beginning of the 14th century (and it seems that the advocates of the older date are prevailing), it is without any doubt that Charles IV knew the legend very well and it is hard to imagine that, knowing the legend, this esoteric ruler and great admirer of the legacy of his Premyslid ancestor would entrust the protection of his new Prague bridge to another saint.

HERALDIC PUZZLES

Many emblems over the tower gate also illustrate the triumphs of Charles IV, which were often political rather than military, but as history shows, the emperor did not hesitate to use arms, if necessary, and usually won. The emblems on the tower demonstrate the expansion of his dominion. In the past, the interpretation of the displayed emblems gave many Czech heraldists a headache. Even the most renowned heraldic authorities failed to identify the feuds of Charles IV.

The current interpretation of their meaning is based on the work of Prague archivist and heraldist Václav Vojtíšek who, in his scientific study, rebutted several errors made by prior interpreters.

In order to read the emblems correctly from a heraldic point of view, we must start with the first emblem on the left from the flower dividing the line of emblems into two parts, i.e. on the heraldically right side. It is the female eagle of the Roman Empire, which is the highest and most prestigious title of Charles IV. On the heraldically left side, there is the second most important emblem — the lion of the Czech Kingdom. By reading the heraldically right and left sides in turn starting from the center, we shall obtain all the remaining titles that Charles IV achieved during his rule: margrave of Moravia, count of Luxembourg, prince of Swidnica, prince of Gőrlitz, prince of Wroclaw, prince of Bautzen, prince of Nisa, and margrave of Lower Lusatia.

We should also mention another emblem on the Old Town Bridge Tower that is usually overlooked. The emblem of Prague, which is in reality the Prague Old Town, is actually on the eastern side of the tower twice. It is probably the oldest existing look of the municipal emblem, which was created by Charles IV. Its even older version — depicted at Wenzelschloss in Lauf, Upper Palatinate, by

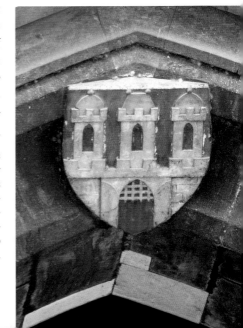

The Prague emblem with archetypal signs of the Celestial Jerusalem was probably first used at the end of the rule of Charles IV. The walls of the city from the Revelation of St. John are made of white gold, there are three towers in each world direction, and the golden gate remains open to indicate that anyone can enter.

The Old Town Bridge Tower, founded after Charles IV's imperial coronation, resembles the triumphal arches of ancient Roman emperors in many respects.

Nurnberg — does not yet have the gate in the wall and the towers have spires instead of hipped roofs.

RENOVATED ROME

Roma caput mundi regit orbis frena rotundi.
Rome holds the reins of the world in its hands.

Leonine verse from the Golden Bull of Charles IV

The Antique motifs in the triumphal adornment of the Old Town Bridge Tower can be traced back to another concept that Charles IV embodied in the foundations of the world's metropolis that he was creating. In addition to the physical image of the Celestial Jerusalem discussed in the book The Prague Horologe, Charles IV's concept of Prague shows some important signs suggesting that he also wanted to make his new royal seat Renovated Rome, *Roma Renovata*.

Actually, the intention to replace the word Rome with the word Prague in the favorite leonine hexameter that used to adorn the crown of Emperor Diocletian and that Charles IV recorded in his Golden Bull as well as on the wall of the audience hall at the castle Karlstein is very obvious in Prague. Charles IV never left his esoteric plans in a state of general proclamations, words, or mere symbols, but materialized them immediately. Thus, they remain for us to see to this day.

As the imperial procession in the Antique Rome walked under the triumphal arch immediately after the emperor performed his ritual cleansing in a bath, the Roman emperor had a bathouse built in Prague near his triumphal arch — the Old Town Bridge Tower. The building right next to Novotného lávka is still there and called the Charles Bathouse even though it lost its original purpose a long time ago. His son Wenceslas made it famous later on thanks to a rather alchemistic legend about the rescue of the young king by bath-keeper Zuzana.

Even though different cities around the world, e.g. Moscow in Russia and Aachen in Germany, claim the title of the "third Rome," it is actually Prague that could have rightfully claimed that title starting in the middle of the 14th century. It was the seat of a ruler who reigned on the "dual throne" and was considered the highest secular and religious authority. He made Prague the back-then third largest city of the world, right after Rome and the "second Rome," Constantinople. He imprinted the genia loci of the sacred New Jerusalem and Renovated Rome in Prague, and thus it is no wonder that Charles IV never really yearned to assume real political power over Rome in Italy even though Italian humanists often asked him to do so. And for the same reason, he obviously never cared to conquer Jerusalem.

KING BY THE GRACE OF GOD

I urge my successors who will be sitting on my dual throne to learn about the two different lives in this world and to choose the better one. In order to better understand it, let's compare it to a face. As the face that we see in the mirror is not a real one, so is not the life of a sinner; it is nothing. This is why Saint John says in his Gospel: "… And without him was not

43

anything made..." But how can an act of a sinner turn into nothing since it was committed? But what he committed was a sin, not an act. This word (opus in Latin) relates to the word desire (optacio in Latin); a sinner desires pleasures, but they stain him. He is wrong in his desire because he yearns for things that turn into nothing. And thus his life is buried with him since when the body dies, so do desires. Saint John says about the other life: "In him was life, and that life was the light of men." And the Savior explains how we can make that life our light: "The man who eats my body and drink my blood shares my life and I share his. The man who eats this bread will live for ever."

Charles IV, Vita Caroli, 1348

The adornment on the western façade of the Old Town Bridge Tower was destroyed by Swedish canons at the end of the Thirty-Year War. We do not have many descriptions or portrayals of the tower from the time prior to this cultural disaster. However, even from the little we know today, we can detect some interesting facts.

Based on one of the existing wood-carvings of Charles Bridge made by J. Kozel and M. Peterle in 1562 that actually shows the western façade of the Old Town Bridge Tower, it is obvious that there was a relief of one of

The wood engraving from 1562, made by Jan Kapr and Michael Petrle, is one of the few pictures of the adornment of the Old Town Bridge Tower destroyed during the Thirty-Year War.

The woman on the destroyed relief on the Old Town Bridge Tower is probably Anne of Swidnica (1339—1362), the third wife of Charles IV and the mother of Emperor Wenceslas IV.

Charles IV's favorite motifs. In front of the Virgin Mary with baby Jesus placed in the center, there was the emperor kneeling on one side and his wife on the other side.

Charles IV had himself portrayed kneeling in front of the Virgin Mary with baby Jesus several times. One of the most expressive portrayals is painted on the wall of Charles IV's private chapel — the Chapel of St. Catherine at the castle Karlstein. This wall painting, however, shows much more than just the ruler paying a tribute to the Savior of mankind. Baby Jesus in the arms of his mother is leaning toward the kneeling emperor, trying to touch his head.

There is no doubt that the painter and the emperor are clearly suggesting in this wall painting that Charles IV's rule and deeds performed in this world have their mission and the blessings of God's son, therefore God Himself. Charles was utterly convinced that this was his role in history.

It is hard to tell how ingeniously the talented Peter Parler approached the tri-dimensional portrayal of the same scene. We will never know what other mysteries and plays of shadows and symbols the initiated ruler and his initiated artist placed on the façade of the Old Town Bridge Tower.

The woman portrayed with Charles on the tower was probably Anne of Swidnica, the third wife of Charles IV whom he married in Buda on 27 May 1353. Anne was the mother of Wenceslas IV, who is depicted with his father on the opposite side of the tower. This hypothesis is supported by the fact that Anne of Swidnica, together with Charles, was crowned Roman empress in Rome on 5 April 1355.

SAINTS ON THE BRIDGE

The predominantly Baroque sculptural adornment along the bridge was not a part of the original concept of the Prague bridge. The bridge first had only a simple cross. A small Calvary was added on across from the cross in the 15th century, but a flood in 1492 tore it down. During the rule of King George of Poděbrady, the king's equestrian statue, a statue of Justice, and a pyramid with a lion and the king's motto *Veritas vincit* (Truth Wins) are believed to have stood in the middle of the bridge. However, this new adornment has gone with the wind, leaving behind no trace and hardly any record. The statue of John of Nepomuk was the first one among today's statues placed on the bridge. It was in 1683. During 1706—1714, the bridge was already adorned with twenty-six statues. More statues were added on much later — during the second half of the 19th century. The last statue placed on the bridge was that of St. Methodius and St. Cyril. It was in 1938.

The first statue among the saints standing on the bridge is that of St. Bernard and the Virgin Mary made by Matěj Václav Jäckel. It is actually this statue, a gift of Abbot Benedict Littwerig of the Cistercian Monastery in Osek from 1709 depicting the father of Gothic architecture, St. Bernard of Clairvaux, that makes us forgive the unbelievable boldness of the Prague Baroque, which tried to complete and somewhat "explain" Charles IV's original ingenious esoteric concept of Prague.

STATUARY OF ST. BERNARD AND THE VIRGIN MARY

Ad Gabrielis Ave respondes optima Fiat. Redde tuum fiat cum repetemus Ave. Dat Bernardus Ave, responde optima Salve. Redde tuum Salve, cum repetemus Ave.
On Gabriel's Ave, you, the best one, answer So Become It! Send your So Become It as we repeat Ave. Bernard says Ave, you, the best one, answer Salve! Send your Salve as we repeat Ave.

Si Gabriel proprium vellet sibi sumere vultum hanc Bernarde tuam sumeret effigiem. Pro Gabrielis Ave recipis Pater optime Salve. Pro nostro Salve redde precamus Ave.

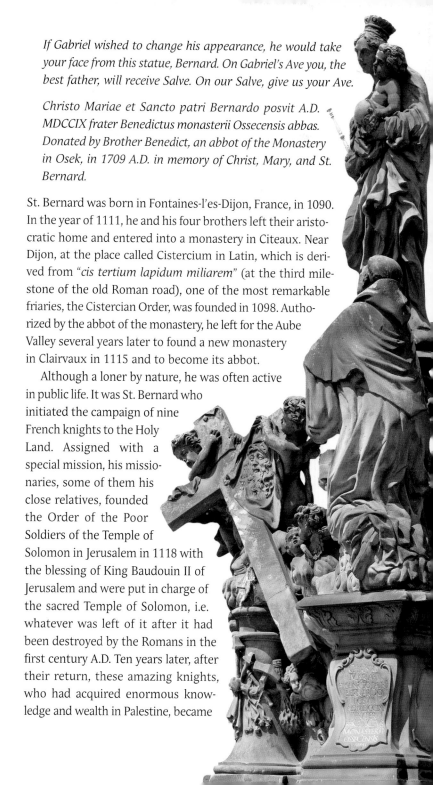

If Gabriel wished to change his appearance, he would take your face from this statue, Bernard. On Gabriel's Ave you, the best father, will receive Salve. On our Salve, give us your Ave.

Christo Mariae et Sancto patri Bernardo posvit A.D. MDCCIX frater Benedictus monasterii Ossecensis abbas. Donated by Brother Benedict, an abbot of the Monastery in Osek, in 1709 A.D. in memory of Christ, Mary, and St. Bernard.

St. Bernard was born in Fontaines-l'es-Dijon, France, in 1090. In the year of 1111, he and his four brothers left their aristocratic home and entered into a monastery in Citeaux. Near Dijon, at the place called Cistercium in Latin, which is derived from *"cis tertium lapidum miliarem"* (at the third milestone of the old Roman road), one of the most remarkable friaries, the Cistercian Order, was founded in 1098. Authorized by the abbot of the monastery, he left for the Aube Valley several years later to found a new monastery in Clairvaux in 1115 and to become its abbot.

Although a loner by nature, he was often active in public life. It was St. Bernard who initiated the campaign of nine French knights to the Holy Land. Assigned with a special mission, his missionaries, some of them his close relatives, founded the Order of the Poor Soldiers of the Temple of Solomon in Jerusalem in 1118 with the blessing of King Baudouin II of Jerusalem and were put in charge of the sacred Temple of Solomon, i.e. whatever was left of it after it had been destroyed by the Romans in the first century A.D. Ten years later, after their return, these amazing knights, who had acquired enormous knowledge and wealth in Palestine, became

 known as the Knights Templars. Even though this order existed in Europe for less than two hundred years, its mystery has been thrilling Europeans to this day.

In the year of 1130, St. Bernard publicly stood up to Antipope Anacletus II, and when in 1145 his pupil Eugenius III became pope, he wrote for him a five-volume elaboration on papal obligations and the principles of a deep spiritual life. St. Bernard received the pope's authorization to call for a second crusade to fight off the Turkish army during the years of 1147 and 1148. However, he was embittered when the crusade failed due to the disagreements and greed of crusaders and a behind-the-back plotting of their leaders.

The quickly spreading mysterious Knights Templars and St. Bernard's Cistecians stood at the birth of the first magnificent edifices of the European Gothic that, as lightening out of the blue, changed the architecture of the Old Continent. Abbot Bernard founded the first early Gothic cathedral in Fontenay already in 1119. The knowledge acquired in the Holy Land, the mystical approach, the spread across the entire continent, and the immense wealth of the Knights Templars brought a completely new approach and energy to European architecture.

"For certainly bishops have one kind of business and monks another. We know that since they are responsible for both the wise and the foolish, they stimulate the devotion of carnal people with material ornaments because they cannot do so with spiritual ones. Art is good for the shallow and ignorant but rather harmful for the wise and perfect. Monks should let the shepherds of people worry about architecture," said St. Bernard.

Perhaps because of these words, lay secular construction guilds became active in construction at the onset of the Gothic style. However, as their predecessors from different religious orders, these free guilds remained relatively exclusive and had their own education and judicial system. They maintained necessary education, enriching it with secret knowledge acquired in the Orient.

Abbot Bernard, called *Magister mellifluus* (Honey-Sweet Master), wrote many elaborations on spiritual life. His sermon on *the Song of Songs* or his writing *De diligendo Deo* (About love for God) are one of the jewels of Christian mystical literature. He died in Clairvaux on 20 August 1153. Twenty-one years after his death, in 1174, he was canonized. In 1830, Pope Pius VIII declared him Doctor of the Church.

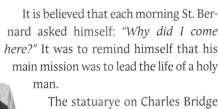

It is believed that each morning St. Bernard asked himself: *"Why did I come here?"* It was to remind himself that his main mission was to lead the life of a holy man.

The statuarye on Charles Bridge refers to the veneration of St. Bernard for the Virgin Mary. He is considered one of the founders and promoters of the Virgin Mary cult in the Western Church. The Virgin Mary holding baby Jesus and the cross on which Jesus died are considerably smaller in size as compared to the statue of St. Bernard.

According to iconographic rules, the difference in size, many heads of angels, and the bare feet of the saint indicate that this is the saint's transcendent vision rather than a real experience.

In addition to the Virgin Mary and the kneeling St. Bernard, sculptor Matěj Václav Jäckel also made the instrument of Christ's martyrdom. The cross, held by two angels, is covered with veraicon, the scarf with which Veronica wiped Christ's face and which bears its imprint. The rooster, backgammon, and the tossed glove of a Roman captain are generally considered the symbols of Christ's martyrdom — the rooster crowed three times when Peter denied Christ, Christ's torturers played backgammon for His clothes, and the soldier's glove hit Christ in the face. The rooster and backgammon are also symbols of France, from where the Cistercian Order came to Bohemia in 1142, i.e. during the life of Abbot Bernard.

The three spikes, pliers, and hammer on the column under the cross can be considered both the instruments of Christ's martyrdom and the symbols of the Cistercian Order that engaged in construction. In Bohemia, the Cistercian Order constructed several architectonically and strategically important monasteries, e.g. in Osek, Vyšší Brod, Zlatá Koruna, and Sedlec near Kouřim. The abbot of the last mentioned monastery, Heidenrich, saw the accession of the Luxembourgs to the Czech royal throne through. And symbolically enough, Gothic art culminated in Bohemia during their rule.

The current statuary on the bridge is a copy of the original. It was made by M. Vajchr, V. Hlavatý, J. and P. Vitvar, M. Tomšej, A. Viškovská-Altmanová, and J. Wolf in 1979. The original is in Gorlice at Vyšehrad.

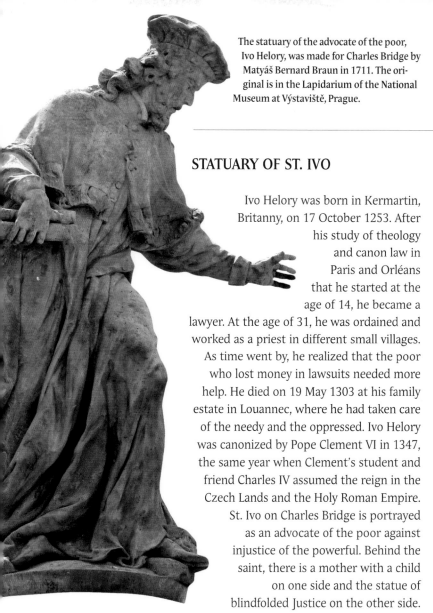

The statuary of the advocate of the poor, Ivo Helory, was made for Charles Bridge by Matyáš Bernard Braun in 1711. The original is in the Lapidarium of the National Museum at Výstaviště, Prague.

STATUARY OF ST. IVO

Ivo Helory was born in Kermartin, Britanny, on 17 October 1253. After his study of theology and canon law in Paris and Orléans that he started at the age of 14, he became a lawyer. At the age of 31, he was ordained and worked as a priest in different small villages. As time went by, he realized that the poor who lost money in lawsuits needed more help. He died on 19 May 1303 at his family estate in Louannec, where he had taken care of the needy and the oppressed. Ivo Helory was canonized by Pope Clement VI in 1347, the same year when Clement's student and friend Charles IV assumed the reign in the Czech Lands and the Holy Roman Empire. St. Ivo on Charles Bridge is portrayed as an advocate of the poor against injustice of the powerful. Behind the saint, there is a mother with a child on one side and the statue of blindfolded Justice on the other side.

The original of the statuary was made by Matyáš Bernard Braun in 1711 and donated by the Law Faculty of Charles University, of which (as well as of all lawyers) St. Ivo is the patron. The current copy was made by František Hergesel Jr. in 1908.

The original is now in the Lapidarium of the National Museum at Výstaviště, Prague.

STATUARY OF THE VIRGIN MARY WITH ST. DOMINIC AND ST. THOMAS AQUINAS

Iesu ac Mariae decori.
For the glory of Jesus and Mary.

Bene scripsisti.
You wrote well.

Ave Maria.
Ave Mary.

Memor esto congregations tvae qvam possedisti ab initio.
Mind the congregation that has been yours since the beginning.

Sancto Thomae Aqvinati Doctori.
To the teacher St. Thomas Aquinas.

Positvs svm ego predicator et doctor in fide et veritate.
I was appointed preacher and teacher in faith and truth.

Sancto Dominico avthori.
To the founder, St. Dominic.

Predicamvus Christvm crvcifixvm ivdeis qvidem scandalvm.
We preach the crucified Christ, which surely offends the Hebrews.

Plantabat predicatorvm religio.
Erected by the Preachers.

Domingo (Dominic) Guzman, a native of Northern Castile, was born in Caleruega, southeast of Burgas, in 1170. As a child, he was strongly influenced by his very religious mother and her brother, a local pastor. He studied philosophy and theology in Palencia, the back-then Leon Kingdom. In 1195, he was ordained and became one of the canons in Osma.

In the year of 1203, Dominic went to Northern Europe for the wedding of the prince of Leon. On his way back, in Languedoc, Southern France, he encountered the Gnostic movement of the Albigensians that the official Church considered heretics. This ascetic sect derived its name from the fortress Albi in Gascony, where it was well rooted already in the late 1170s. The Cathars (the Pure), called Albigensians in Southern France, criticized the overly rich Church and kept attracting more and more people, including

---

◁ The original Baroque statuary from 1708, made by Václav Matěj Jäckel, which is currently in the Lapidarium of the National Museum at Výstaviště, was replaced by a copy made by V. Bartůněk and S. Hanzl in 1961.

noblemen and burgesses. According to their dualistic teachings, people were of angelic origin and later became trapped in the material world by the devil. The road to redemption was in liberation from material things. Man had to voluntarily give up all secular, material things. They abhorred clergymen and called Rome the "Whore of Babylon" and Roman bishops "Anti-Christs."

Dominic spent eight years in Béziers, Narbonne, Carcassonne, Toulouse, and other towns of Southern France trying, together with the Cistercians, to convert the Albigensians to Catholicism by wearing poor clothes and walking barefooted. However, Catharism was solid. It stemmed from the ancient tradition of Gnostic teachings about pure life without sin and it is believed that the Cathars of Languedoc guarded the secret of the Holy Grail at their Montségur Castle, which Joseph of Arimathea and Mary Magdalene, a friend or perhaps the wife of Jesus, had brought there after their flee from Palestine following the death of Jesus Christ.

In the year of 1211, Innocent III, feeling threatened by the Albigensian faith, called a crusade against the heretics in Southern France. About twenty thousand cavalrymen and ten times more infantrymen participated in the crusade. Papal legate Arnald Amalric made his mark in history by giving his answer to a soldier's question of how to distinguish the Albigensians from the Catholics. He commanded: *"Kill them all. God will know his own."* The slaughtering in Languedoc unleashed by the crusaders remained practically the biggest massacre in history, in proportion to the back-then European population, until the middle of the 20th century. The Albigensians and other adversaries of Rome were literally wiped out. Just during the plundering of Béziers with the Cathedral of St. Mary Magdalene, twenty thousand people — including women, children, and the old — were killed. The total number of victims of the fifteen-year massacre in Languedoc exceeded one hundred thousand people. A horrid number for that time! The Albigensians did not defend themselves since they were pacifists. Hardly anybody survived, and the demographic growth in Southern France has not recovered from it to this day. However, Montségur Castle has not released its secret. It is believed that the Holy Grail was saved at the last minute from the conquerors and hidden in an unknown place.

Dominic first went into seclusion. It is believed that during that time he was helping people by putting in a good word for them with Catholic authorities. However, he refused the bishop office in Béziers and accepted instead the office of general vicar in Carcassonne. In the year of 1215, Dominic acquired the house of a rich burgess in Toulouse, which was now free of the Albigensians, and turned it into a monastery, the center of a new order, based on which science and discipline were to help to raise teachers and preachers. The rules of the new order were based on those of St. Augustine and included some rules of the Premonstratensians. In Toulouse, Dominic built the first large Dominican monastery. Pope Honorius III gave him permission to found the new order, and, a year later, called his members *Praedicatores*, Preachers. The order became the main tool of the Catholic inquisition in this region and later on in the entire Europe.

Dominic died in Bologna on 6 August 1221. He parted with his brothers saying: *"Do not cry, I will be more useful to you after my death than alive."* It is believed that twelve years after his death, his body was still intact and many people were miraculously cured by his grave. This is why Pope Gregory IX canonized Dominic already in 1234, saying that this man *"who was a saint during his life and blessed by the Virgin Mary shall be forever worshipped as one of the foremost saints."*

Four years after Dominic's death, in 1225, an Italian theologian and philosopher, *Doctor Anglicus*, Tommaso d'Aquino, was born at Roccasecca Castle by Aquino. He was the son of a relative of the Hohenstaufen imperial family of Count Landulph of Aquino. He spent his childhood at the Benedictine Abbey of Monte Cassino and studied liberal arts at the University of Naples.

Against the wishes of his family, he left for Paris where he studied with the German monk, scholar, and alchemist Albert the Great, whom Thomas Aquinas respected his whole life. After three years of his studies in Paris, he followed Albert the Great to Cologne on Rein so that he could study with him for another four years. He returned to Paris in 1252, where he started teaching theology.

When Thomas Aquinas became a theologist of the papal court in Orvieto, Italy, he met Dominican William of Moerbeke, who translated many writings of Aristotle from Greek to Latin. Using these translations, Thomas continued with the work of Albert the Great, who studied Aristotle's writings from Arabic translations. Returning to Paris during the years of 1269—1272, Thomas Aquinas became the most famous theology teacher of that time. He discussed all controversial issues, solving many of them by the force of his authority. He died as a prominent religious figure in the abbey in Fossa Nove situated between Naples and Rome.

After his death, his teachings became the official philosophy of the Dominican Order even though some parts of his teachings were soon prohibited e.g. at the University of Paris in 1277. His followers were even persecuted. His teachings were revived at the beginning of the 14th century thanks to his canonization by Pope John XII in 1322. In the year of 1879, they became the official philosophy of the Catholic Church, and their modernized version has been dominating in the Catholic Church to this day.

The statuary of the spiritual fathers of the Dominican Order was ordered by the Convent of the Dominican Order at the Church of St. Giles in the Prague Old Town and made by sculptor Matěj Václav Jäckel one year before he completed the Cistercian statuary with St. Bernard right next to it. The statuary portrays the Virgin Mary holding baby Jesus and giving prayer beads to St. Dominic. The legend says that St. Dominic received prayer beads from the Virgin Mary, who also taught him the rosary and asked him to spread this prayer as a way of giving faith to the lost.

Thomas Aquinas, with a book, quill, chain with the shining Sun, and angel with a beehive, looks at the scene. Under the Virgin Mary, there is the earth in clouds and a symbolic dog with a torch in his mouth, which is to remind us that the Dominicans used to be called the Dogs of the Lord. Before Dominic was born, his mother had a dream about a faithful dog of the Lord, and the burning torch became the symbol of the Dominican Order.

STATUARY OF ST. BARBARA, ST. MARGARET, AND ST. ELIZABETH

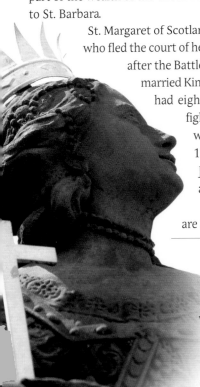

Orate pro nobis nvnc et in hora mortis. IOAN BRO-KOFF FECIT.
Pray for us now and in the hour of our death. Made by Jan Brokoff.

St. Barbara is a frequently mentioned saintess. The daughter of nobleman Dioscorus probably lived in Nicomedia, today's Turkey, in the 3rd century. In order to protect her from Christianity, her father shut her in a tower. However, the girl was receiving Christian visitors in secret and accepted the Christian faith, for which she was then tortured and sentenced to death by beheading. Dioscorus himself carried out the death sentence. According to legend, on his way home he was struck by lightening.

Barbara became the patron of many professions, in particular of miners. It is no wonder that one of the most beautiful Czech Late Gothic cathedrals built in Kutná Hora, the city with silver mines that represented a substantial part of the wealth of the Czech Lands in the Middle Ages, was consecrated to St. Barbara.

St. Margaret of Scotland (1045—1093) was a native of Hungary, who fled the court of her uncle Edward the Confessor in England after the Battle of Hastings in 1066. Four years later she married King Malcolm III of Scotland, with whom she had eight children. She became well known for fighting old Celtic traditions and rituals. She was canonized by Pope Innocent IV in 1249. Her glory was fostered mainly by the Jesuits, who have been keeping her head at Douai to this day.

As there are several St. Margarets, there are also several St. Elizabeths in the pantheon

The statuary of Barbara, Margaret, and Elizabeth is a somewhat anachronical and heterogeneous group of Catholic saintesses. However, it is no exception on Charles Bridge. Similarly to other statues made by the Brokoff workshop, the work was signed by the father, Jan Brokoff, even though the statues were often made by his sons. ▷

of more than five thousand Catholic saints. In Prague, the most famous St. Elizabeth is St. Elizabeth of Hungary, sometimes also called Elizabeth of Thuringia. The daughter of King Andrew II of Hungary was born in Bratislava, Upper Hungary, in 1207. At the age of 14, she married Count Ludwig IV of Thuringia, who died six years later on a crusade.

The widowed Elizabeth left everything and joined the Order of St. Francis, where she took care of the poor. It is rather interesting that Elizabeth's confessor was Conrad of Marburg, who abused her both physically and psychologically. It is no wonder that she died young, at the age of twenty-four. The year she died, Pope Gregory IX conferred on Conrad of Marburg the extensive authority of the first grand inquisitor of the Holy Church. Conrad immediately started terrorizing all heretics. His motto "I would gladly burn a hundred innocent people if there was one guilty person among them" shows the fanatism of this inquisitor.

Conrad of Marburg was beaten to death in 1233 by a relative of one of the victims. Paradoxically enough, two years later the same pope, who appointed Conrad the head of inquisition, canonized one of his first innocent victims, St. Elizabeth. The church in Marburg, consecrated to St. Elizabeth, was the first Gothic edifice in Germany.

The statuary of the three saintesses was donated to Charles Bridge by Imperial Councilor and Associated Justice Jan Václav Obytecký of Obytec in 1707. It comes from the Brokoff family's workshop. According to the inscription under the statue of St. Barbara, the entire monument was created by Jan Brokoff. However, art historians believe that the actual statues were made by his son Ferdinand Maxmilian and only the pedestal was made by the father.

CALVARY — STATUARY OF THE HOLY CROSS

Kadoš, Kadoš, Kadoš, Adošem Cevaot. Restavratvm ao MDCCVII.
Holy, holy, holy Lord of the masses. Renovated in the year of 1707.

Trognásobně Svatý, Svatý, Svatý, ke cti Krista Ukřjžovaného z pokuty proti
křjži rouhagicího se žida od slawného Králowského Tribunalu Apellatio-
num. Založené Léta Pánie 1696 dne 14. zářj.
Triple holy, holy, holy, for the glory of the crucified Christ. Paid for from
a fine that the reputable royal court charged to a Jew blaspheming the
cross. Founded on 14 September 1696 A.D.

Carolo Adamo baroni de Rziczan, qvi perpetvvm hoc
lvmen et sacrvm perpetvvm metropolitano sacello
divi Wenceslai fvndavit, legato bono lavniowicz sedi
archiepiscopali ioannes fridercvs archiepiscopvs pra-
gensis hoc monvmentvm posvit A.
MDCLXXXI.
Donated by Prague Archbishop Jan
Bedřich in 1681 in memory of Baron
Karel Adam of Říčany, who founded
this eternal light and mass in the
Metropolitan Chapel of St. Wenceslas
and generously bequeathed Louňovice to
the archbishopric.

Jesus Christ on the cross is the oldest adornment of the
bridge balustrade between the two bridge towers. It was
already there during the life of Charles IV, practically since
the very beginning, and there is an interesting legend about
its placement.

According to old records,
in 1361 there was a certain
dispute between Old Town
councilors and the priest
Martin Cinek. The coun-
cilors decided to radically
resolve the entire matter.
Even though the priest
did not fall under their

jurisdiction, they sentenced Martin Cinek to death and the mob actually threw him off the bridge into the Vltava River. However, such a willful act angered the Prague archbishopric since it infringed its rights, and the dispute had to be settled by the king.

The cross was erected in memory of the murdered priest at the place where he was thrown into the river. A part of this story is also in the writings of the canon of the Prague Church and the chronicler of Charles IV, Beneš Krabice of Weitmühle, who says that Archbishop Ernest of Parbudice finally gave the guilty an absolution for seven thousand strychs (ancient square measure) of wheat for the poor and two eternal lights for the Church of Hradčany.

> *In the same year, since the crop was bad everywhere, wheat was very expensive, one strych of wheat actually cost half a threescore in Prague, and many thousands of people starved to death and others died of the plague that was still raging. Provoked by the devil, the reeve and councillors of the Old Town stuck the priest Martin from the Prague Church in a sack and drowned him in front of people. When the emperor heard about this deed, he became very angry, removed all those who participated in the crime from their office, and refused to enter the Old Town until they all were gone.*
>
> Beneš Krabice of Weitmühle, 14th century

This report is interesting for two reasons actually. First of all, the construction of the bridge had to be rather advanced four years after its foundation since people threw the dead man's body into the river at the place of the cross, which is right in the middle of the river. The second aspect of this story is important from a historical point of view. Three hundred twenty-two years later, a second statue was added to the Stone Bridge and was also dedicated to the memory of a priest allegedly thrown into the Vltava River — John of Nepomuk. As we will see later on, the famous legend about John of Nepomuk contains many deliberate and indeliberate lies, half-truths,

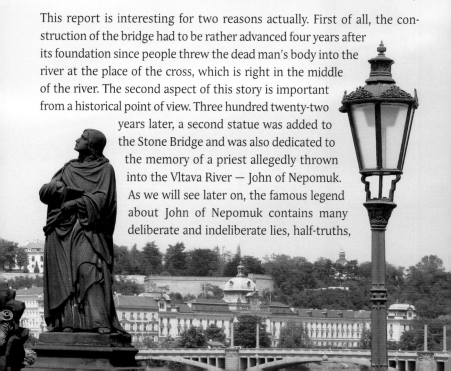

and misinterpretations, which in the end caused the Roman Church to canonize a man who never lived and thus never died.

The similarity of John of Nepomuk's death and that of the priest Cinek, who however was never canonized, casts a shadow of doubt even on that part of Nepomuk's life that so far nobody has dared to doubt, i.e. how he died and whether he was actually thrown into the Vltava River. Let's not forget that these two similar events happened only thirty years apart.

The statuary of the Holy Cross has changed its look several times during its long existence. The original cross was perhaps destroyed by the Hussites in the year of 1419 and was not replaced until the second half of the 15th century. The cross with the wooden body of Jesus Christ from 1629, accompanied with St. John, the Virgin Mary, and St. Mary Magdalene painted on boards, was destroyed during the fight of the Prague people against the Swedish army in 1648. Then, for a short time, there was a color carving of the Calvary made by Jeremiáš Fischel and Fabián Harovník. The current bronze and gilded body of Jesus Christ was bought from Hillinger merchants in Dresden in 1657 for 500 thalers, the fine of Bohuchval Valkoun of Adlar, the lord of Zlonice. Between the years of 1666 and 1861, there were two lead statues made by bell-founder Mikuláš Löw of Löwenburk, which were then replaced by sandstone statues of the Virgin Mary and John the Evangelist made by Emanuel Max.

As the trilingual inscription on the statue says, the gilded inscription in Hebrew around Christ's body was made in 1696 and paid for with the fine of a Jew who sneered at the cross. However, since today's tourists do not understand the trilingual inscription and find it scandalous to have one in Hebrew next to the Son of God, the Prague municipal office had an explanation sign in Hebrew, Czech, and English placed on the balustrade of the bridge at the beginning of the 21st century.

STATUARY OF PIETA

O vos omnes, qui transitis per viam, atendite et videte si est dolor sicut dolor meus.
O all you who pass this way, look and see whether there is any sorrow like my sorrow.

Em. Max inv. et fecit.
Designed and made by Emanuel Max.

In 1695, the statuary of Pieta made by sculptor Jan Brokoff was erected at the place where Calvary used to be starting in the 15th century. In 1859, the rather deteriorated statuary was replaced by another one with the same theme created by Emanuel Max.

Traditionally, the scene shows the Virgin Mary holding the dead body of Jesus Christ. His mother and closest disciples — John the Evangelist, who witnessed and recorded the crucifixion at Golgotha, and St. Mary Magdalene — cry over Jesus.

The last two mentioned figures in particular are interesting from the point of view of esoteric Christian tradition. As discussed in detail in the book The Prague Horologe, many findings of occult research of bible history indicate that the author of the fourth New Testament Gospel, i.e. the witness of the crucifixion and the "favorite disciple," was not John but Lazarus, to whom Jesus offered high mysterious initiation. His sister was Mary Magdalene who, in the Gnostic tradition, enjoys the exclusive position of the "Apostle of the Apostles" and the closest follower of Jesus Christ (contrary to the deeply rooted Catholic myth of a "repented prostitute").

Non-canonical, i.e. apocryphal, gospels put this exclusive position of Mary Magdalene above the teachings that the remaining disciples received from Jesus. In particular, the Gospel of Philip mentions that Jesus often kissed Mary Magdalene on her mouth, which makes many scholars in the last decades think that Mary Magdalene was Jesus's lover, wife, and even the mother of His children. The advocates and opponents of this non-traditional interpretation of the legacy of Mary Magdalene have been disputing to this day.

◁ The statuary of Pieta, made by Emanuel Max, is in the place where Calvary used to be in the 15th century.

STATUARY OF ST. ANNE

The story of St. Anne, mother of the Virgin Mary, and her husband Joachim is more known from legends than canonical gospels. According to legends, Anne was already too old to bear a child when she conceived Mary. An angel from heaven supposedly announced to Anne and her husband Joachim the birth of a child, as he later on announced to Mary the birth of Jesus Christ.

The statuary created by Václav Matěj Jäckel in 1707 and paid for by Count Rudolf of Lisov, the lord of Nový Stránov and Vtelno, shows the saintess together with her daughter Mary and grandson Jesus, which is her most typical portrayal — the so-called Anne Selbdritt "Herself Making a Third," the maternal version of the Trinity. The symbol of St. Anne in alchemy is also a metaphor of the Great Mother, a womb where everything originated. As to this traditional Christian portrayal of the holy family, we would like to mention that the Austrian scholar and founder of anthroposophy Rudolf Steiner — who transcendently researched the spiritual phenomena of the life and death of Jesus Christ from the so-called Akashic Chronicle, the spiritual chronicle of the history of

St. Anne Selbdritt is the oldest statuary made by Václav Matěj Jäckel for Charles Bridge. Similarly to other statues, the statuary on the bridge is a modern copy. The original is in Gorlice at Vyšehrad.

Rudolf Steiner (1861—1925) was an Austrian scientist who systematically studied the spiritual aspects of human existence. He was one of the co-founders of the German branch of the Theo-sophical Society. After its dissolution, he founded his own Anthroposophical Society. He studied the philosophical aspects of spiritual reality and focused on their practical use in social and education systems and areas of regular life. He wrote several books and gave many presen-tations that his students recorded in books.

the world encoded in the etheric of the earth — found out that the description of all events captured in the canonical gospels was extremely accurate. It is actually so accurate that two different authors of two different gospels writing about the origin and childhood of Jesus clearly speak of two different people!

In fact, Matthew and Luke, connected to the same source of inspiration as Rudolf Steiner, describe two different family trees of the child Jesus. The former derives Jesus's origin from King David's son Solomon[2] while the latter derives it from King David's son Nathan.[3] Thus there are two similar, yet not quite identical, versions of the birth and childhood of Jesus. In his writings, Rudolf Steiner describes how, long before Jesus Christ's baptism in Jordan and public appearance, these two people and families merged from a spiritual point of view.[4]

[2] Mt 1,1–17

[3] L 3,23–38

[4] The description of what happened would far exceed the scope of this book, and therefore I would like to refer anyone interested in this issue to the extensive writings of Rudolf Steiner, in particualr his lectures on the Gospel of John, Luke, Matthew and Mark and his book, the Fifth Gospel. All these books have been published in many world languages.

Jan Brokoff presents St. Joseph on Charles Bridge as a carpenter standing on a beam. The blooming stick in his hand may refer to the apocryphal tradition, which says that he was chosen as the husband of the Virgin Mary by the blooming stick. However, the lily-type blossoms may also refer to the purity of their relationship, as Church iconography likes to indicate, or to the coming of God to the Earth, which was symbolized in Antique mysteries by lilies.

STATUE OF ST. JOSEPH

Zum andenken gewidmet von Josef Berg-mann Bürger und Kaufmann in Prag.
Donated by Josef Bergmann, a Prague burgess and merchant, in memory of St. Joseph.

Both gospelers describe two different family trees of Jesus to arrive to King David as mentioned by prophecies. And even if they rigorously follow the father's line, Church tradition considers the closest male ancestor, St. Joseph, a mere foster-father. The biblical legend says the only reason why he did not leave his pregnant wife was the revelation of an angel.[5]

Although Joseph was of royal origin, the same tradition considers Joseph a carpenter. There are two early Christian writings that talk about the father or foster-father of the Savior in detail. The so-called Protogospel of James from the 2nd century and the History of Joseph the Carpenter from the 4th century mention that when Joseph became engaged with Mary, he was a widower with children. Historians have not yet satisfactorily unraveled the complicated tangle of Jesus's family, based on existing sources. However, in the 1620s Pope Gregory XV declared the celebration of the Feast of Joseph (19 March) mandatory. Therese of Avila and the founder of the Jesuit Order, Ignatius of Loyola, were great promoters of Joseph's cult.

The original statue of St. Joseph made by Jan Brokoff in 1706 was damaged during the uprising of 1848, removed from the bridge, and placed in the Lapidarium. The current statue of St. Joseph was made by Josef Max in 1854.

[5] Mt 1,20—21

STATUARY OF ST. CYRIL AND ST. METHODIUS

Brothers Michael and Constantine came from a prominent family of one of the senators in Salonika, Greece. Michael was probably born in 825 and Constantine one or two years later. They both studied at the University of Constantinople, where they later on taught philosophy.

However, their road to fame started differently. Michael became a governor of the Macedonian province and Constantine was ordained deacon and worked as a librarian at the Church of Hagia Sophia in Constantinople. In 856, Michael renounced public life and went to live in a monastery on Mount Olympus by Constantinople. He changed his name to Methodius. His brother Constantine joined him four years later.

Emperor Michael III, later on called the Drunkard, remembered both educated brothers and sent them to Russia in 861 to convert the Khazar Jews. They learned the local dialects and traveled to the wilderness between the Don River and the Caucasus Mountains. Their mission was very successful; they even found the relics of the fourth Roman Pope, St. Climent. Thus, when in 863 Michael III decided to meet the wish of Prince Rostislav of Great Moravia to send a Christian mission, he turned to both brothers again.

Constantine and Methodius took advantage of their Slavic origin after their mother and thoroughly prepared for the mission. Constantine even invented an alphabet called glagolic that consisted of 38 letters and was derived from the Greek alphabet. They translated the Bible, liturgical writings, the psalmbook, the missal, and other religious texts into glagolic. They thus laid the foundations for the Slavonic language, which became the fourth Christian liturgical language after Latin, Hebrew, and Greek. Their diligent preparation paid off again — their mission was a success and the Cyrillic alphabet derived from Constantine's glagolic has been used by many Slavic nations to this day.

The three-year mission of the brothers from Salonika in Great Moravia was resented by Catholic neighbors who claimed the right to work in the region. In 867, Pope Nicolas I summoned both brothers to Rome because they were promoting the Scripture in an unapproved language. But Nicolas I died and was succeeded by Adrian II, who simply approved the Slavonic liturgy by the Bull from 868.

The physically weak Constantine, who took the name Cyril, decided to stay in Rome while the pope appointed Methodius the papal legate and archbishop of Pannonia and Moravia. Shortly after, Cyril died in Rome on 14 February 869, had a grand funeral attended by the pope, and was buried in the Basilica of St. Clement whose relics he actually had brought to Rome. Methodius, heading for the new place of his mission at the junction of the Danube River and the Sava River, was captured and imprisoned by Alvin, the archbishop of Salzburg, who claimed the right to Methodius's office.

Pope John VIII arranged for Methodius to be released, but it was just the beginning of disputes between the missionary from Byzantine and the Catholic clergy in the region. The Slavonic liturgy was first prohibited, then the pope set up a separate Church province for it. Methodius had problems both with Church prelates, who accused him of Greek heresy, and with secular authorities. After his death on 6 April 885, all his followers were chased out of Great Moravia. Eleven years later, the Slavonic liturgy was definitely prohibited by Pope Stephan VI.

In the 11th century, St. Prokop, trying to preserve the Slavonic rite in the Czech Lands, founded the Monastery of Sázava; however, even this initiative did not last long. Charles IV was a little bit more successful. In the year of 1347, he founded the Slavonic Emmaus Monastery in Prague (Na Slovanech) and brought Slavonic monks there. Charles IV, a great collector of relics of saints, also acquired several relics of St. Cyril from Rome for the St. Vitus treasure. We do not know what happened with the relics of Methodius. Archeologists have been searching in vain for his grave in Moravia to this day.

The statuary of St. Cyril and St. Methodius is the youngest statue on Charles Bridge. It was created by sculptor Karel Dvořák during 1928—1938 and donated by the Ministry of Education and Culture. It is in the place where there used to be a statue of the founder of the Jesuit Order, Ignatius of Loyola, made by Ferdinand Maxmilián Brokoff that fell into the Vltava River during a big flood in 1890. The original statue was lifted from the bottom of the river, put together, and is now exhibited in the Lapidarium at Výstaviště in Prague.

The statuary of Cyril and Methodius, made by Karel Dvořák, is the youngest statue on Charles Bridge. The Byzantine brothers are still considered to be the first people to bring Christianity to the Czech Lands even though Christian missions from Western Europe, even from Ireland, had worked in this territory long before the two brothers came here. However, Cyril and Methodius baptized powerful ruling families and thus their mission was much more successful than the previous ones. The statuary is in the place where there used to be a statue of the founder of the Jesuit Order, Ignatius of Loyola. ▷

STATUARY OF ST. FRANCIS XAVIER

Sancto Francisco Xaverio S. I. indiarvm et japoniae apostolo theosopho geminae facvltates theologica et philosophica vniversitatis pragens posvere MDCCXI.

Donated by the Faculty of Theology and the Faculty of Philosophy of the Prague University in 1711 in memory of Francis Xavier from the Society of Jesus, a God-enlightened apostle of Hindus and Japonese.

Francisco de Jaso y Azpilcueta was born in Navarro, Spain, in 1506. He studied at the University of Paris, where he befriended Ignatius of Loyola. In the year of 1534, they and other five brothers founded the Jesuit Order at Montmartre, of which he later on became the second general.

Francis Xavier was assigned missions, in particular in India, Malaysia, and other nearby regions. He also tried to convert the Japanese who, however, thanks to the several thousand years of spiritual tradition of Hinduism and Buddhism, were not interested in Christianity. His new tactics, i.e. replacing his poor missionary clothes, in which he tried to convert the poor, with expensive clothes to convince the rich, did not help either.

After his failed mission in the Land of the Rising Sun, he set out for China to spread Jesuit ideals, but died suddenly in a wooden shack on the Island of Sancian near Canton in 1552. His remains are in the Born Christ Church in Goa, which used to be his base during his missions in India. He was canonized by Pope Gregory XV in 1622.

The statuary on Charles Bridge commemorating the missions of the second general of the Society of Jesus was ordered by two faculties of the Prague University and made by Ferdinand Maxmilián Brokoff, who was only twenty-three years old at that time. The face of the boy holding the biretta (priest's cap) on the book is actually the face of the young sculptor. During the big flood in 1890, the statuary fell into the Vltava River and was retrieved piece by piece during 1892—1904. In the year of 1913, sculptor Vincenc Vosmík made a copy of the statuary for Charles Bridge based on the assembled original, which is now in the Lapidarium at Výstaviště in Prague.

The statuary of Jesuit General Francis Xavier, as well as that of Ignatius of Loyola, fell into the Vltava River during a flood. Both reconstructed monuments can now be seen in the Lapidarium at Výstaviště. Another interesting thing about the statuary of Francis Xavier, the exact copy of which is still on the bridge, is that it shows a self-portrait of the twenty-three-year-old sculptor Ferdinand Maxmilián Brokoff. ▷

STATUE OF ST. JOHN THE BAPTIST

We can read about John the Baptist in the New Testament. According to gospeler Luke,[6] John was born to Elizabeth, the wife of the priest Zechariah, who was considered barren. Elizabeth was a relative of the Virgin Mary, and it was archangel Gabriel who announced to her that she would give birth to a son.

As an adult, John carried out his ministry in the Judean desert dressed only in a camel skin. He washed away the sins of his followers by baptizing them in the Jordan River. This is also where Jesus was baptized by him at the beginning of his ministry described in the gospels.

Based on some indications in the gospels and research findings of many scholars, John's ministry was closely connected with the teachings of the Essenes, a Jewish mystic sect. The Essenes created exclusive communities in Palestine before the birth of Jesus Christ and engaged in the teachings of the ancient Egypt and Jewish prophets that were passed on verbally and in writing. The Essenes were very knowledgeable in astronomy and astrology, went through several levels of initiation, and their religious teachings were deeply affected by the anticipated birth of the Messiah.

It is believed that Elizabeth, the mother of John the Baptist, belonged to the Essenes, who lived in towns and did not join the monastic communities. Actually, it is obvious that Jesus Christ had close contacts with the Essene culture and was influenced by it. After Jerusalem was conquered again in 69, the mysterious sect vanished. Many Essenes were murdered, others fled and found a new home around the world. The very first worshippers of Jesus Christ were recruited mostly from the Essenes. Their original Gnostic approach is reflected in many esoteric Christian teachings of the first and second millenniums.

Spiritual scholars consider John, who received an education in Essene monasteries, to be the reincarnated Jewish prophet Elijah, which is also supported by the words of Jesus Christ in the Gospel of Matthew: "For all the prophets and the Law prophesied until John. And if you care to accept it, he himself is Elijah, who was to come. He that has ears to hear, let him hear."[7]

---

[6] L 1,36; [7] Mt 1,13—15

Even John's death has this karmic connection. During the rule of King Ahab, the prophet Elijah had all priests of the god Baal, whose worshipping had been introduced in Israel by the wife of King Ahab, Jezebel, killed. Jezebel swore revenge to the prophet. The revenge came in the illegitimate wife of King Herod, Queen Herodias. She persuaded her daughter Salome, who had danced for the king, to ask for the head of John. King Herod fulfilled her wish and had John beheaded. The head was then brought on a dish and presented to the girl.

The statue of John the Baptist on Charles Bridge, made by Josef Max and donated by Jan Norbert Gemerich of Neuberk, replaced the statue of the Baptized Lord made by Jan Brokoff in 1706, which was quite damaged during the fighting in 1848 and therefore removed in 1855.

The statue from 1857, made by Josef Max, represents John the Baptist as a simply dressed man leaning against the cross and showing the right way. His non-traditional pose is also enhanced by a scallop-shell attached to his waist, a typical symbol of pilgrims traveling to the grave of James the Great in Santiago de Compostela.

STATUE OF ST. CHRISTOPHER

Ut ille nos pelago saeculi jactatos bracchio potenti perducat ad portum salutis quem mirum infantem felix Christophore pie portasti per fluctus te coelestem periclitanitum in undis patronum cives precamur pragenses.

May His mighty arms carry those who are being tossed in the sea of centuries to the haven of salvation as you, lucky Christopher, lovingly carried the miraculous child through waves. This is the prayer of the citizens of Prague to You, the heavenly patron of those who risk their lives in waves.

Cleri pragensis duces et cultores viribus unitis pouerunt.
Donated jointly by the Prague clergy and venerators.

Anno reparatae salutis MDCCCLVII die festa S. Christophori.
In 1857, the year of renewed salvation, on the holy day of St. Christopher.

E. Max invenit et fecit 1857.
Designed and made by E. Max, 1857.

It is believed that St. Christopher was born as pagan Offerus in Canaan in the 2nd century A.D. The golden legend says that he was of an extraordinary size and strength and his pride was such that he vowed that he would serve only a master who was more fearsome than himself. He first served an earthly master, but learned that the master was afraid of the Devil. Thus, he pledged himself to the Devil's service, only to abandon him when he learned during one of his journeys that the Devil was in turn afraid of the cross of Jesus. So he left the Devil and set out in search

The statue of the giant Christopher with baby Jesus on his shoulder stands where the sentry-box of the local garrison used to be. During a flood in 1784, several soldiers, who did not have enough time to escape, drowned.

of this even more powerful king. During his search, Offerus encountered a hermit and inquired as to how he could serve Jesus. The hermit directed him to a swift river and suggested that Offerus carry people across the river on his back. Offerus did as he was told. One stormy evening, a small child approached the river and asked to be carried across. When they reached the middle of the river, huge waves started coming and the child seemed heavier and heavier. Offerus yanked out a large tree to get support, yet he felt that this time he would not be able to take the load all the way to the other side of the river. He said to the little boy: "If I had the whole world on my shoulders, it could not be heavier than you are." The child responded: "You should not be surprised, you have on your shoulders the entire world and the one who created it."

When Offerus, carrying Jesus, finally reached the other side of the river, Jesus baptized him and gave him a new name, Christopher (Christo-phoros in Greek, which means the carrier of Christ).

For the homophony of the Greek words *Christos* (Christ) and *Chrysós* (gold), the scene with the child carried across the river became a favorite symbol of alchemists, to whom it expresses young aborning gold that is carried over the stormy mercurial wet essence.

Even the legendary death of the saint giant was not a simple matter. Two hundred soldiers armed with bows and arrows were not able to kill him, and therefore another two hundred had to be called. The legend about Christopher says that he who sees the saint's image shall not die that day. This is why his cult became very popular even though it was often criticized by Church authorities as well as by Erasmus of Rotterdam in his Praise of Folly.

The statue of St. Christopher, the patron of travelers, stands in the place that used to be reserved for a long time for the sentry-box of the local garrison. However, during a flood in 1784, water undermined the pillar under the sentry-box which, together with five soldiers, fell into the river.

In the year of 1720, Count F. A. Špork planned to put a statue of Emperor Charles, made by his protégé Matyáš Bernard Braun, on the roof of the sentry-box, but the project did not materialize. The statue of St. Christopher with Jesus, created by Emanuel Max and donated by the Prague magistrate Václav Wanka and the Prague clergy, was placed on the bridge on 24 July 1857.

STATUARY OF ST. NORBERT WITH ST. WENCESLAS AND ST. SIGISMUND

Honori divi Norberti patriarchae sacri ac canonici ordinis praemonstratensis atque patroni regni bohemiae anno salutis MDCCCLIII tertio iam posuit venerandasque ss. regum Venceslai et Sigismundi imagines adiunxit laetis sub auspiciis reverendisimi ac magnifici Hieronimi Zeidler praesulis Sionei canonia strahovensis.

Donated by Jeroným Zeidler, an abbot from Strahov, for the third time in 1853 with the statues of St. Wenceslas and St. Sigismund, in memory of St. Norbert, a holy patriarch and canon of the Order of Premonstratensians and a patron of the Czech Kingdom.

S. Venceslavsm. Dvxet patronvs Bohemiae decvs solamenaqve patriae.
St. Wenceslas. A martyr, Czech prince and patron, the grace and consolation of the country.

S. Sigismvndvs M. Rex Burgundiae patronvs Bohemiae regni Christi propvgnator perennis.
St. Sigismund, a martyr. A king of Burgundy, Czech patron, and eternal warrior of the Kingdom of Christ.

Ios. Max inv. et fecit
Designed and made by Josef Max.

Norbert, the second son of the count of Gennep, was born in Xanten, the Rhine region, sometime around the year of 1080. Thanks to the good standing of his family and the back-then practices of filling high offices, Norbert, still a boy, was appointed canon at the Church of St. Victor.

The intelligent, educated, and noble Norbert was summoned as an almoner to the imperial court of Henry V. During the time of disputes between Henry V and Pope Pascal II regarding the right for lay investiture (confirmation of clerics by a lay ruler), Norbert traveled with Henry V to Rome, which his benefactor conquered, and actually opposed him when Henry V put the pope under house arrest. Later on, in 1113, Norbert even refused Henry's offer of a well-paid lay investiture of a bishop in Cambrai, Northern France.

Two years later, after having been struck by lightening near Wreden in Westphalia, Norbert joined the Benedictine Monastery in Siegburg and was ordained priest. Following this sudden conversion, he traveled a lot and found many supporters. After he met with Pope Gelasius II in Languedoc, Cathar, and at the synod in Reims, he and his thirteen pupils founded a new order in a "foreshown place" — Praemonstratum — in the Prémontré Valley, northwest of Reims. The first Premonstratensians took their vows in 1120.

In the year of 1126, Norbert was elected archbishop of Magdeburg by the pope and was always involved in the political life of the Church and the Holy Roman Empire. Two years later, he joined a crusade of Emperor Lothar II to Rome in defense of Pope Innocent II against Analectus II. The

◁ The statuary of three patrons of the Czech Lands celebrates mainly the youngest of them, the founder of the Premonstratensian Order, Norbert of Gennep. He quickly became a part of the pantheon of Czech saints during the Thirty-Year War. He is buried at the Strahov Monastery, which can be seen from the statuary.

emperor appreciated his involvement in this matter by appointing him imperial chancellor for Italy. He died shortly after his return from Rome to Magdeburg and was buried in the local Premonstratensian church. The founder of the Premonstratensian Order was canonized by Pope Gregory XIII in 1582.

In the year of 1626, after a special military action of the army of the Habsburg Catholic Emperor Ferdinand II during the Thirty-Year War, the saint's relics were moved from Magdeburg to Prague. Kašpar of Questenburg, an abbot of the Premonstratensian Monastery at Strahov, was very much involved in negotiations with Protestant Saxons. The saint's relics have remained in this Prague monastery, founded in 1142, to this day.

While the relics of St. Norbert were being transported, Count Ernst of Harrach, the Prague archbishop, quickly made Norbert one of the Czech patrons. The statuary on Charles Bridge made by Josef Max in 1853 is to remind us of it because there he stands between St. Wenceslas and St. Sigismund. The Premonstratensians from Strahov and Abbot Vít Seidl had the original statuary of their founder placed on the bridge already in 1708, but the statuary, made by Jan Brokoff, showed St. Norbert with St. James and St. Adrian rather than with the Czech patrons Sigismund and Wenceslas. In the year of 1765, it was replaced by another statuary — St. Norbert with angels — made by Ignatius Platzer Senior.

We will see a separate statue of St. Wenceslas on the bridge later on. St. Sigismund is not here only once either. He and St. Adalbert are a part of the group of statues on the façade of the Old Town Bridge Tower.

Sigismund of Burgundy was the son of Gundobald, the Vandal king of Burgundy in the 5th century. He first confessed the teachings of the priest Arius of Alexandria that were very popular in the 4th century but condemned by the First Council of Nikaea as heretical, contradicting true Christianity.

Influenced by Bishop St. Avitus of Vienne, Sigismund officially converted to Roman Christianity and founded a monastery dedicated to Saint Maurice in Agaune, Valais, in 515, where he had the relics of the legendary holder of the Holy Spear, St. Maurice, and other Christian martyrs moved from the Roman Theban Legion.

In the year of 516, Sigismund became the king of Burgundy. After a political dispute, his second wife wanted his son Sigerich dead. The king finally succumbed to her pressure and had his son strangled. According to legend, he immediately realized his mistake. Overcome with remorse, he retired to the monastery that he had founded and spent the whole time praying to atone for his sin.

When the Franks invaded Burgundy in 523, Sigismund led his army, but lost the battle and Burgundy. Although he put on a monk's habit and hid in a cell near his abbey, he was captured, taken to Orléans, and drowned in a well, together with his wife and other two sons.

Twelve years after his death, Sigismund's relics were taken to St. Maurice and acquired by Charles IV for the Cathedral of St. Vitus in the second half of the 14th century. Its largest bell still bears the name of Sigismund.

STATUARY OF ST. FRANCIS BORGIA

Ioannes Brokoff fecit.
Made by Jan Brokoff.

The Jesuit saint, Francisco de Borja y Aragón, came from the infamous family of Borgia. His grandfathers were Pope Alexander VI and King Ferdinand V of Aragon. Francis was born in 1510 and dedicated the first half of his life to a secular career (he was even a viceroy of Catalonia) and heaping up riches. In 1547, after the death of his wife and mother of eight children, he joined the Society of Jesus.

Francis Borgia's career in the Jesuit Order was as steep as the secular one. In the year of 1554, the founder, Ignatius of Loyola, named Francis Borgia commissary-general of the order in Spain and Portugal. Eleven years later, he became the third general of the order, and, as such, founded new provinces and colleges and sent his militant Catholic brothers on missions to recatholize the entire Europe and conquered colonies. He was so zealous that he has been considered the second founder of the Jesuit Order.

Francis Borgia died in Rome in 1572, and ninety-nine years later, was canonized by Pope Clement X.

The statuary of the Jesuit general was paid for by the imperial burgrave Franz of Collet and made by twenty-two-year-old Ferdinand Maxmilián Brokoff in 1710, who got inspiration for his work in the actual center of the Jesuit Order, the "Gesú Nuovo" Church, which Francis Borgia had built. The angel on the side of the saint was modeled after the angel on the alter of St. Ignatius in the Church of St. Ignatius in Rome.

The third general of the Jesuit Order, Francis Borgia, is a typical representative of the "repented sinner," whose servile service to the Catholic Church even made him a saint. The statuary, inspired by the Italian Baroque, was ordered by the imperial burgrave Franz of Collet and made by the young Ferdinand Maxmilián Brokoff.

STATUE OF ST. JOHN OF NEPOMUK

*Divo Ioanni Nepomvcenno anno MCCCLXXXIII
ex hoc ponte deiecto erexit Mathias L. B. de
Wunschwitz anno MDCLXXXIII.*
Donated by Baron Mathias of Wunschwitz in
1683 in memory of St. John of Nepomuk, who
was thrown off this bridge in 1383.

Brokoff fec.
Made by Brokoff.

Me fecit Wolff Hieronymvs Heroldt in Nvremberg 1683.
I was cast by Wolf Jeroným Heroldt in Nurnberg in 1683.

John of Pomuk was born to a family of the reeve Wolfin in 1340 in the village called in turn Pomuk or Nepomuk that belonged to the nearby Cistercian Abbey on Zelená hora. He studied in the local parish school and then at the University of Prague, where he received his bachelor degree in law.

Starting in 1369, John of Nepomuk first worked in Prague as a scribe in the office of Archbishop Jan Očko of Vlašim and then as an imperial notary, an alter boy of the Vlašim Chapel in the Cathedral of St. Vitus, and a vicar of the Church of St. Gallus. In the year of 1383, he signed up for four-year studies in canon law at the University of Padua. After his return to Prague, John of Nepomuk, a fresh graduate from the renowned university, held canon positions at the Church of St. Giles and at Vyšehrad and very quickly became the vicar-general of the Archbishop of Prague, Jan of Jenštejn.

In the 1390s, the Prague archbishopric was in feud with King Wenceslas IV over the right to fill offices; they both claimed the right. The feud culminated

---

John of Nepomuk is probably the most popular statue among the visitors of the Czech capital. Every day, the statue is surrounded by hundreds of tourists who, for some unknown reason, have lately started touching the reliefs showing the saint's alleged life for good luck. However, according to an old Prague legend, it is the small metal cross in the balustrade, at the place where the saint was thrown into the Vltava River, that has the magical power to make anyone's wish come true. All one has to do is put the fingers of one hand on the five stars of the cross (see above), to make a wish and not tell it to anybody.

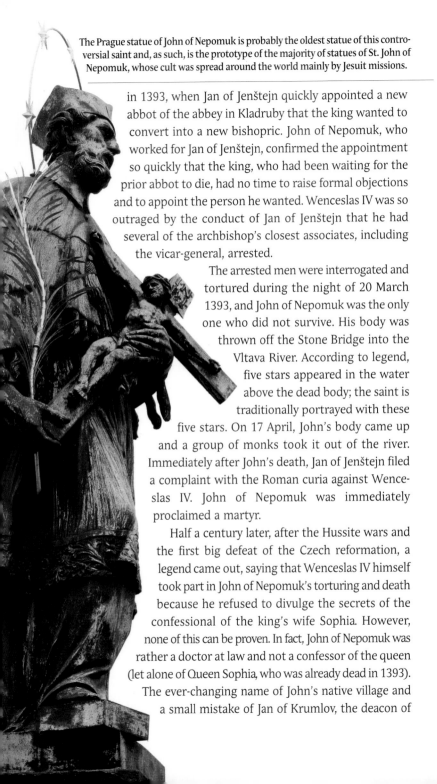

The Prague statue of John of Nepomuk is probably the oldest statue of this controversial saint and, as such, is the prototype of the majority of statues of St. John of Nepomuk, whose cult was spread around the world mainly by Jesuit missions.

in 1393, when Jan of Jenštejn quickly appointed a new abbot of the abbey in Kladruby that the king wanted to convert into a new bishopric. John of Nepomuk, who worked for Jan of Jenštejn, confirmed the appointment so quickly that the king, who had been waiting for the prior abbot to die, had no time to raise formal objections and to appoint the person he wanted. Wenceslas IV was so outraged by the conduct of Jan of Jenštejn that he had several of the archbishop's closest associates, including the vicar-general, arrested.

The arrested men were interrogated and tortured during the night of 20 March 1393, and John of Nepomuk was the only one who did not survive. His body was thrown off the Stone Bridge into the Vltava River. According to legend, five stars appeared in the water above the dead body; the saint is traditionally portrayed with these five stars. On 17 April, John's body came up and a group of monks took it out of the river. Immediately after John's death, Jan of Jenštejn filed a complaint with the Roman curia against Wenceslas IV. John of Nepomuk was immediately proclaimed a martyr.

Half a century later, after the Hussite wars and the first big defeat of the Czech reformation, a legend came out, saying that Wenceslas IV himself took part in John of Nepomuk's torturing and death because he refused to divulge the secrets of the confessional of the king's wife Sophia. However, none of this can be proven. In fact, John of Nepomuk was rather a doctor at law and not a confessor of the queen (let alone of Queen Sophia, who was already dead in 1393). The ever-changing name of John's native village and a small mistake of Jan of Krumlov, the deacon of the St. Vitus Canonry, who had recorded the year of 1383 as the year of John's death, led the historian Václav Hájek of Libočany to an allegation that there were actually two martyrs — John of Pomuk and John of Nepomuk. One of them was supposedly drowned in 1383 because he had refused to divulge the secrets of the confessional while the other one died ten years later due to the feud over the abbey in Kladruby. In the year of 1680, Jesuit Bohuslav Balbín, a

renowned Czech historian, used this information from Václav Hájek's Czech Chronicle (1541). It was no wonder that, in the second half of the 17th century, the Jesuits first very much opposed the canonization of this saint.

However, the bronze statue of John of Nepomuk, designed by Jan Brokoff and cast by Wolf Jeroným Heroldt in Nurnberg, has been on the bridge since 1683. Its votive inscription mentions the year of 1383 as the year of the saint's death, which is wrong. When the saint's remains were exhumed in 1719, a piece of reddish tissue fell out of his skull. It was believed to be his tongue that did not divulge the secrets of the confessional, but the analysis conducted in the 20th century showed that it was brain tissue.

On 31 May 1721, Pope Innocent XIII proclaimed John of Nepomuk blessed, and on 19 March 1729, Pope Benedict XIII proclaimed him a saint. Historians agree that the saint, whom the Church canonized, was the person that Václav Hájek of Libočany and Bohuslav Balbín had described as John of Nepomuk, drowned in 1383 because of the secrets of the confessional. Even though, shortly after, Eliáš Sandrich rebutted Václav Hájek's error and proved that the legend about the confessional was

rather gossip that was meant to damage the reputation of the king, it was impossible to stop the spreading of the mystery of John of Nepomuk. Jesuit missions from the nearby Clementinum made him famous in Europe and around the world. Thus, we can see St. John of Nepomuk with his typical attribute of five stars around his head on many bridges throughout the world that this man, who never actually lived, is to protect.

STATUE OF ST. LUDMILA

In Czech legends and myths, St. Ludmila is always mentioned in connection with her grandson, St. Wenceslas, whom she raised. Ludmila was born to the dynasty of prominent pagan princes of Pšov in the Mělník region sometime around the year of 860. As a fourteen-year-old girl she was married to the Premyslid Prince Bořivoj II. A year later, she gave birth to her oldest son, Spytihněv, who later on became a Czech prince.

Bořivoj II was the first Czech prince to be baptized. It is believed that he was baptized by a legendary Slavic missionary, Archbishop Methodius, in Velehrad in the 870s. Later on, Methodius baptized Ludmila as well. By converting to the Christian faith, the Premyslids gained political supremacy over other tribal princes in the Czech

Matyáš Bernard Braun did not make his statue of St. Ludmila directly for Charles Bridge. The statue contains a small mystery, which is the demolished column on which the grandmother of St. Wenceslas is stepping. The remains of the reliefs on the column probably indicate the destruction of pagan cults by this first Czech Catholic Princess.

Lands. Bořivoj II, the husband of Ludmila, was also the first Premyslid ruler to move his seat from Levý Hradec to Prague.

After the death of her husband in the year of 889, Ludmila became active in political life and participated in the rule of her sons Spytihněv (875—915) and Vratislav (888—921). During the rule of Vratislav, she also helped to raise her grandsons Wenceslas and Boleslav. A dispute between Ludmila and her daughter-in-law over guardianship after Vratislav's death drove Ludmila to

The original of the statue of St. Ludmila made by Matyáš Bernard Braun is now in the underground casemate Gorlice at Vyšehrad; the statue on Charles Bridge is a copy.

86

seek sanctuary at Tetín Castle, near Prague.

However, the influence of the old Ludmila, who lived to the respectable age of sixty, was a threat to the power of Princess Drahomíra, who eventually had Ludmila strangled. The legend of St. Ludmila says that she was strangled with her own scarf at Tetín Castle by Viking soldiers Tunna and Gommon during the night on 15 September 921. She was originally buried at the castle, and since people witnessed miracles by her grave, Drahomíra decided to build the Church of St. Michael there.

In 925, the young Prince Wenceslas had the relics of his beloved grandmother moved to the Church of St. George at the Prague Castle. During the rule of Boleslav II, a Benedictine monastery for women was added to the church. Ludmila was canonized in 1144.

The statue of St. Ludmila with her grandson, an angel, and a relief depicting the death of St. Wenceslas was made in the workshop of Matyáš Bernard Braun. It was created sometime after the year of 1720 but was not placed on the bridge until after 1784, when the statue of St. Wenceslas, made by the foremost sculptor of Roman Baroque in Prague, Ottavio Mosto of Padua, in the 1690s, fell off. The original of the statue made by Ottavio Mosto is in the Lapidarium.

STATUE OF ST. ANTHONY OF PADUA

Deo incarnato et sancto Antonio de Padva erigebat et dicabat C. M. V.
Erected and dedicated to incarnated God and St. Anthony of Padua by Kryštof Moric Wittauer.

Dei gloriae zelotes hostes Iosephi Caesaris feri timore.
The zealot of God's glory, make the enemies of Emperor Joseph tremble with fear.

It is believed that even fish listened to Anthony's preaching. Painting by Spanish painter José Benlliura y Gil (1855–1937).

Fernando de Bulloes y Taveira de Azevedo was born to a rich noble family in Lisabon in 1195. At the age of fifteen, he joined the Canons Regular of St. Augustine and later on the Santa Cruz Monastery in Coimbra. There he was very much moved by the returned bodies of five Franciscan monks tortured to death during their mission in Morocco. He joined the Franciscan Abbey in Coimbra and took the new name of Anthony, under which he worked as a missionary among pagans. However, in the desert he became gravely ill and had to go back to Europe.

After having been ordained in Portionucelle by Assisi, he left to preach in Northern Italy and Southern France, where the Catholic Church was fighting the Cathars. He is believed to have preached there to crowds of ten thousand people. However, another legend about St. Anthony says what was really happening in the proud region of the Albigensians. When nobody listened to his preaching at least he held the attention of fish sticking their heads out of the water. Whether Anthony of Padua talked to people or fish, at any rate Pope Gregory IX awarded him for his preaching with the title "the Ark of the Covenant." However, he was also known under the nickname "the Hammer of Heretics."

During the years of 1227 — 1230, Anthony was elected minister provincial of the Franciscan Order in Northern Italy. He died in 1231 by Padua at the age of thirty-six. For his fighting against heretics, he was canonized by Gregory IX only eleven months after his death, which is unheard of. Gregory IX also canonized St. Dominic and St. Francis of Assisi.

The statue, made by Jan Oldřich Mayer in 1707, shows the scenes from the legend about the saint. The statue was donated to Charles Bridge by Kryštof Mořic Withauer, the councilor of the Prague Castle.

STATUARY OF ST. FRANCIS SERAPH

Sancto Francisco Seraphico ob Franciscum Iosephum Imperatorem Av-
gvstvm MDCCCLIII divinitvs servatvm D. D. Franciscvs Antonivs comes
Kolowrat Liebsteinsky eqves avrei velleris MDCCCLv.
Donated by Count František Antonín Kolowrat Libštejnský, a knight of
the Order of the Golden Fleece, in 1855 in memory of St. Francis Sera-
ph for the miraculous salvation of Emperor Franz Joseph in 1853.

For he will command his angels concerning you to guard you in all
your ways. Psalm 90,11.

Em. Max inv. et fecit.
Designed and made by Emanuel Max.

Giovanni di Bernardone was born to the family of a rich merchant from Assisi, Pietro di Bernardone, in the 1180s. His original name was John. He took the name Francis later on. As a young man, he participated in several crusades in back-then unstable Italy, during which he actually spent about a year as a hostage.

During one of the crusades he had a vision that he communicated with the crucified Christ. Because of the vision, he sold a large portion of merchandise without his father knowing it and donated the proceeds to a church for repairs. After the consequent fight with his father, Francis became a hermit. Later on, around 1210, he founded the Order of Friars Minor — the Franciscans — and traveled around the world, going all the way to Palestine.

He never stopped having visions of the crucified Christ. His claim to fame is that he is probably the first person in history showing so-called stigmas, blood marks on the body exactly in the same places where Jesus Christ suffered his wounds. Francis had these stigmatic imprints after his vision of a crucified seraph with six wings on 12 September 1224; however the Franciscans did not discover them until after the saint's death. Since then, tens of more or less famous people have supposedly experienced similar miraculous marks.

Francis died in his native town of Assisi in 1126 and was canonized by Gregory IX only two years after his death.

Today, the original statuary, made by sculptor and inn-keeper František Preiss of the Lesser Town in 1708 and paid for by art benefactor Václav Vojtěch of Šternberk, is in front of the church of the Capuchin Friars Minor. The statuary on Charles Bridge, made by Emanuel Max, was ordered by Count František Kolowrat Libštejnský.

Francis of Assissi on the statuary made by Emanuel Max is accompanied, similarly to his visions, by seraphs.

STATUE OF ST. JUDAS THADDEUS

Apostle Judas Thaddeaus was one of the closest disciples of Jesus Christ. The statue, made by Jan Oldřich Mayer, shows him with a club, with which he was beaten to death during his preaching in Persia.

Devoto Christi Amico.
To the devoted friend of Jesus Christ.

The Baroque statue of Judas Thaddeus with a club in one hand and a book in the other, made by Jan Oldřich Mayer in 1708, is a typical portrayal of this disciple of Jesus Christ. He is similarly depicted in the procession of the Apostles made by Vojtěch Sucharda on the Old Town Horologe. The book in his hand is the symbol of the Apostles and shows us that Judas Thaddeus was the author of one of the Epistles of the New Testament. The club in his other hand is to remind us of his death, since he is believed to have been clubbed to death somewhere in Persia.

Judas Thaddeus is considered to be the "brother of the Lord," the younger brother of Apostle James the Less. However, it is also believed that he was not a Jew, but the son of a foreign king. Similarly to Apostle Peter, Judas Thaddeus was married and had children. He was probably the first one out of the close circle of Jesus's followers to leave Palestine. He gospeled, usually with Apostle Simon, in Arabia, Mesopotamia, Syria, Armenia, Phenicia, and Persia.

The statue with the inscription "To the devoted friend of Jesus Christ" was donated to Charles Bridge by František Sezima, the knight of Mitrovice, Nemyšle, and Jetřichovice.

STATUARY OF ST. VINCENT FERRER AND ST. PROKOP

S. S. Vincentio Ferrerio et Procopio binis patronis D. D. D.
To both patrons, St. Vincent Ferrer and St. Prokop

Convertit 100 000 peccatores.
He converted 100 000 sinners.

resuscitavit 40.
He resuscitated 40 people.

8000 saracenos ad fidem catholicam.
He converted 8 000 Saracens to the Catholic faith.

2500 iudeos ad christum.
He converted 2 500 Jews to Christ.

70 daemones domuit.
He tamed 70 demons.

Timete Deum et date illi honorem qvia venit hora iudicii eius.
Fear and honor God since the hour of His judgment is coming.

Opvs Ioanis Brokoff.
Work of Jan Brokoff.

Vincent Ferrer was born in Valencia in the year of 1350. At the age of seventeen, he entered the Dominican Order and soon became famous as an excellent preacher. He was called by the papal court to Avignon, where he spent some time as a chancellor and confessor of Pope Benedict XIII.

Vincent Ferrer was a contemporary of Czech Church reformer John Hus, but the two of them had a rather different view of spiritual needs. While John Hus further developed the reformatory

Spaniard Vincent Ferrer and the Czech abbot Prokop are presented by Ferdinand Maxmilián Brokoff as a thaumaturgist and a tamer of devils. One of the reliefs actually shows the famous legend about the harnessed devil ploughing the field.

ideas of John Wyckliff, Dominican Vincent preached fiercely against heretics. During the Council of Constance that had John Hus burnt at the stake in 1415, Vincent Ferrer spoke against Benedict XIII. In order to resolve the great schism in the Roman Catholic Church — during which there were two, and later on three, rival popes — Vincent urged Benedict XIII to resign, but to no avail. Therefore Vincent arranged for the pope to be removed from power.

Vincent spent the last three years of his life preaching in Brittany and Normandy, France, where he also died in 1419. He was canonized in 1455 by Pope Calixtus III, who used to be called Alfonso de Borja and to whom Vincent Ferrer had foretold a papal tiara in Valencia a long time ago.

Prokop, the founder of the Sázava Monastery, was born to the family of a yeoman in Chotoun sometime around the year of 970. He studied at the school of St. Peter at Vyšehrad, and even though he is believed to have been married and to have had a son, Jimram, he became a priest and monk. He most likely took religious vows at the Benedictine Monastery in Břevnov, founded by Bishop Adalbert Slavnik in 993.

After the slaughter of all Slavniks, he and several other brothers left the monastery; however, contrary to them, he did not look for a refuge abroad, but became a hermit in a cave in Dalejice by Jinonice. In this cave, Prokop supposedly wrote a gospel-book that somehow got to France and on which French kings used to take their oath.

Starting in 1009, he moved to the woods by the Sázava River where he continued his life of a hermit. According to legend, people saw him ploughing with the devil harnessed to a plough and propelled by a cross. A monastic and hermitical settlement of his followers started to grow around his hermitage, among which were also his own son Jimram and nephew Vitus. Monks always gathered to pray together in the Slavonic liturgy brought to the Czech Lands by St. Cyril and St. Methodius. With the help of Prince Oldřich and Prince Břetislav, this group then turned into a monastic community with the Western rules of St. Benedict and the Eastern Slavonic liturgy. Prokop became its first abbot and died there on 25 March 1053.

Since his canonization by Pope Innocent III in 1204, St. Prokop has become one of the Czech patrons. In the year of 1588, Prokop's remains were moved to Prague and placed in the Church of All Saints at the Prague Castle.

The sandstone statuary, made by Ferdinand Maxmilián Brokoff and donated by Remedius Josef František, Count Thun, the lord of Choltice, was placed on Charles Bridge in 1712.

STATUE OF ST. AUGUSTINE

Jan Bedřich Kohl created the statue of the Church father, the reformed Manichaean Aurelius Augustine, for Charles Bridge in 1708. The little angel by his feet is to remind us of Augustine's words that man will pour the sea over with a shell before he will understand God. The burning heart is the typical attribute of this saint. The original statue is in Gorlice at Vyšehrad.

Doctorvm principi.
To the prince among teachers.

Doctorvm principi magno religio-
num patriarchae divo patri
Avgvstino pietas filialis erexit.
Erected by his proud sons in
memory of the prince among
teachers, the patriarch of the
Church, St. Augustine.

The originally confirmed, but later on reformed, Manichaean Aurelius Augustine of Hippo is still considered one of the Church fathers. He was born in Tagaste near Carthage, Northern Africa, on 13 November 354 to a pagan father, Patricius, and a Christian mother, Monica, who was later proclaimed a saint.

St. Augustine was an excellent speaker. He learnt rhetorics in Milan, Madaura, and Carthage and studied Antique authors such as Plato, Vergilius, and Cicero. As a young man, he lived a very prodigal life and had an illegitimate son with his mate, Melany. Augustine became a zealous follower of the Gnostic teachings of the Persian Mani, who lived in the 3rd century and felt destined to carry on a religious and moral renovation of mankind. These teachings were very popular at that time and competed with the so-far weak official Roman Church.

Augustine turned 180 degrees at the age of twenty-three after his alleged mystical visions. His mother, Monica, who never stopped trying to convert him to the "true faith," and Bishop Ambrose in Milan surely played some role in this turning point of his life. He rejected his illegitimate mate and had himself and his son baptized.

On a certain day within the holy octave of Easter, when in the morning many brothers, Christian lay people, came and sat down as usual, we began to talk about the Christian religion, comparing it to the power of thinking and seemingly great divination of pagans. I have written down the conversation for others, without mentioning the names of those who, although Christians, disputed each other; it almost seemed that in their arguments, they searched for answers appropriate for pagans. When the divination of demons was examined and someone said that the downfall of the Temple of Sarapis in Alexandria had been foretold, I replied that one should not marvel that demons could know and predict that downfall was impending their own temples and images, and other events, also, in so far as it is allowed to them to know and announce it.

Aurelius Augustinus: De divinatione daemonum

After his conversion to Roman Christianity, Augustine returned to Algeria and devoted his life to forming an ascetic religious community. He wrote over a hundred books and two hundred letters, in which he philosophically turned away from his former heresy and created the foundations of an uncompromising official Christian doctrine. In Hippo he was first ordained and, at the age of forty, became bishop. He founded a monastery that followed strict rules based on asceticism and poverty, which later on gave rise to the Augustinian Order. The teacher of the Church, St. Augustine, died in Hippo on 28 August 430 during a year-long siege of the city by Vandal King Genserich. After the Vandals conquered the city, the fleeing Christians took his remains with them to Sardinia and then to the Church of St. Peter in Ciel de Oro in Pavia.

In 1708, the Prague Convent of the Augustinian Order by the Church of St. Thomas commissioned sculptor Jan Bedřich Kohl to make the statue of its founder.

FIDeLIVM
CONSOLATOR

STATUE OF ST. NICHOLAS OF TOLENTINO

Fidelivm consolatori.
To the consoler of the faithful.

Divo Nicolao de Tolentino prodigiosa sangvinis emanatione paneqve benedicto miracula continva patranti (sacrvm).
To St. Nicholas of Tolentino, who made miracles with exuded blood and blessed bread.

In the year of 1245 in Sant' Angelo by Ancona, a long-desired son was finally born to middle-aged Compagnonus de Guarutti and his wife Amata de Guidiani. They named him Nicholas after St. Nicholas of Myra, at whose grave they used to pray for a child.

As his mother had promised, 18-year-old Nicholas joined the Augustinian Order. He became a priest, preached, traveled to different monasteries, lived as a hermit, and became famous for his miraculous healing of the ill. As a thirty-year-old priest, he came to Tolentino where, according to a revelation from heaven, he was to spend the rest of his life. He got immediately involved in local political fights between the supporters of the pope and those supporting the emperor, but also healed the ill.

Nicholas died in Tolentino on 10 September 1305 after a long illness. It is believed that he continued making miracles even after his death. During the first twenty years following his death, people who came to his grave witnessed over three hundred miracles. It is believed that during important Church events, his arms, severed from his body, bled at least twenty-five times. The inscription on the statue on Charles Bridge reminds us of this phenomenon. Nicholas of Tolentino was canonized by Pope Eugene IV in the year of 1446.

As a great promoter of the Virgin Mary, Nicholas of Tolentino is usually portrayed in an Augustinian habit with a lily in his hand and "Saint Nicholas Bread" that supposedly had healing effects after he distributed it while praying to the Virgin Mary. His statue, made by Jan Bedřich Kohl in 1708, depicts him with a lily in his hand and an angel holding a basket with Saint Nicholas Bread.

◁ Jan Bedřich Kohl captured Nicolas of Tolentino with his typical symbol, Saint Nicolas Bread. This bread supposedly had healing effects, as shown by the inscription on the angel's basket. The original statue is in Gorlice at Vyšehrad.

STATUE OF ST. CAJETAN

*Qvaerite primo regnvm Dei et ivstitiam eivs et haec omnia adjicientvr
vobis. Math. Cap. 6. v. 33.*
*But seek first his kingdom and his righteousness, and all these things will
be given to you as well. Matthew 6:33.*

*Sanctvs Caietanvs Thienaevs clericorvm revlarvm fvndator apostolicae
vivendi formae imitator.*
*St. Cajetan the Theatine and the founder of the order, who lived the life
of an apostle.*

Ioan. Brokoff fecit et invenit.
Designed and made by Jan Brokoff.

The founder of the Theatines (Cajetanians), Gaetano dei Conti di Tiene, was
born to a famous and rich noble family in Tiene, Italy, in October 1480.
He studied theology and law at the University of Padua and was ordained
in 1516.

Cajetan understood the need to reform Church practices and was
involved in establishing lay and religious fraternities. In the year of 1523,
he assisted Giovanni Pietro Craffa, an anti-Semite and grand inquisitor, and
Pope Paul IV in establishing the Congregation of Clerks Regular in Rome.
The congregation members were either called the Cajetanians after their
founder or the Theatines after Chieti (Theate), the diocese of which Caraffa
was the bishop. Pope Clement VII confirmed the congregation in 1524.

Cajetan worked in Verona, Venice, and Naples, where he then moved the
seat of the Cajetanians in 1527 after the imperial army had plundered Rome.
The Theatines created a network of pawn-shops to help the poor. Later on,
some of them became modern banks.

Cajetan died in Naples sometime in 1547 and is buried in the Church of
S. Paolo Maggiore. He was canonized by Pope Clement X in 1671.

Thirty-eight years after, in 1709, the Prague Convent of the Theatines
paid 774 guldens and 45 kreutzers for the statue of St. Cajetan resembling
an obelisk covered with clouds and the heads of angels and topped with a
sacred heart representing the Holy Trinity. The statue was probably made
by Ferdinand Maxmilián Brokoff, the son of Jan Brokoff.

The Theatine Order was founded by St. Cajetan, together with Giovanni Pietro Craffa, the grand
inquisitor and anti-Semite, and Pope Paul IV. However, the statue resembling an obelisk,
made in the Brokoff workshop, points out a somewhat nicer part of the saint's life. ▷

The masterpiece from 1720, made by Matyáš Bernard Braun, captures the mysterious scene from the vision of the blind Cistercian nun, Luitgarda. His work was well received and Braun was given a chance to create many extremely valuable statues in Bohemia, including those for Charles Bridge. ▷

STATUARY OF ST. LUITGARDA

S. Lutgardis ordinis cisterciensis.
Donated by the Cistercian Order in memory of St. Luitgarda.

Vivificum latus exugit cor mutuans corde. Ex brev. cist. ad XV. iunii.
The vivified side gave a heart for another heart. From the Cistercian breviary for 15 June.

Christi crucifixi constricta branchi.
Embraced with the arm of the crucified Christ.

D. honori S. Lutgardis posuit monasterium de plass ord. cisterc. svb evgenio tyttl abbate et praeposito S. M. Magd. ad Boh. Lippam MDCCX.
Erected by the Cistercian Abbey of Plasy in 1710 during the office of Evžen Tyttl, an abbot and provost of the Church of St. Mary Magdalene in Česká Lípa, in honor of St. Luitgarda

In the year of 1194, a beautiful twelve-year-old girl, Luitgarda of Tongeren by Lutych, the Netherlands, was sent to the Benedictine Abbey of St. Catherine in Saint Trond because her parents lost everything, and a girl without a dowry had practically no chance to get married.

In the abbey, she became very withdrawn. During her adolescence she had many visions, levitations, and other mystical experiences. In the year of 1205, she actually became an abbess, but three years later left the abbey to join the community of Cistercian nuns in Aywieres by Brussels. She stayed there more than thirty years and used her unusual gift to heal the ill and to communicate spiritual experiences. She was blind the last eleven years of her life, still having her visions. In one of her last visions, Jesus Christ told her when she would die. It happened in Aywieres on 16 June 1246. Her relics have been in Bas-Ittre, Brabant, since 1827.

The statuary on Charles Bridge captures one of her mystical visions, in which the crucified Jesus leaned toward her and let her kiss his bleeding wounds. Sculptor Matyáš Bernard Braun made the statue for the Cistercian Abbey of Plasy in 1710 for 1 200 guldens. The statuary is one of the best works of art on Charles Bridge.

STATUE OF ST. PHILIP BENIZI

*Phillippvs Benitivs ordinis servor-
vm B. V. M. quintus generalis in hu-
militate placvit Deo.*
*St. Philip Benizi, the fifth pri-
or-general of the Servants of Mary,
was loved by God.*

The parents of the Italian Philip Benizi were aristocrats Giacomo Benizi and Albaverde Frescobaldi from
Florence. Philip was born on the day
the Servites founded their order in
Florence — 15 August 1233. He received an excellent medical and
philosophical education in Padua
and Paris and earned a doctorate at
the age of nineteen. After a year-
-long medical work experience, he
decided to follow his vision of the
Virgin Mary. He joined the Order of
Servites and started studying theology. On 5 June 1267, he became the
fifth prior-general of the order. He
codified the Servite rules and founded a female branch of the order.

In the year of 1268, he was named
as a potential papal candidate, which
was so distressing to Philip that he
fled and hid on Mount Tuniato until
Gregory X was elected pope. He died
with a cross in his hand in a Servite
house in Todi on 22 August 1285.
His remains and death mask made

The statue of Philip Benizi made of Salzburg marble was created by one of the
most prominent Austrian Baroque sculp-
tors, Michal Bernard Mandel. The tiara by
the saint's feet is meant to remind us that,
in 1268, Philip refused his papal candidacy.

of wax are in Todi.

The statue that the Prague Convent of the Servites ordered in 1714 from
the famous Baroque sculptor Michal Bernard Mandel in Salzburg, Austria,
is the only marble statue on Charles Bridge.

STATUE OF ST. ADALBERT

Marcvs de Ioanelli, regiae Anti-qvae Vrbis pragenae consvlaris pvblico cvltvi exposvit.
Erected by Marcus de Joanelli, a councillor of the Prague Old Town, to publicly honor St. Adalbert.

Vojtěch, who came from the Slavnik dynasty that settled in Libice and was the main rival of the Premyslids in the power struggle over the Czech basin, was born around the year of 956. He was raised by priests in his native town of Libice. In the year of 972, he left to study in Magdeburg, where this talented student spent nine years. After his return to Bohemia, the young Vojtěch worked with

The statue, made by Josef Michal Brokoff, depicting St. Adalbert is a Baroque variation of the same saint made by Peter Parler on the Old Town Bridge Tower. While Parler's original is in the Lapidarium at Výstaviště, Prague, Brokoff's original statue is in Gorlice at Vyšehrad. Both statues of St. Adalbert on the bridge are copies.

the first Czech Bishop Dětmar. After the bishop's death, he was confirmed by Bishop Adalbert of Magdeburg in Levý Hradec in February 982 in the presence of Premyslid Prince Boleslav II and was appointed bishop. Vojtěch is known abroad under the name of Adalbert, which he was given at his confirmation.

Adalbert was noted for zealously fighting paganism, alcoholism, polygamy, and slave trade. However, his enthusiastic struggle for Christian ideals in the harsh conditions in Bohemia of the 10th century lasted only until 988 when, disgusted, he and his brother Radim left Prague and Bohemia to see Pope John XV in Rome. In Italy, he lived in several monasteries (Monte Cassino, Valle Luca, and Aventino) and took monastic vows.

Adalbert did not return to his diocese until he received a message from Boleslav in 992. He took with him several Italian monks with whom he founded a monastery in Břevnov, which was the first male monastery in Bohemia. However, he did not stay in Prague for a long time. In 994, he left his diocese for good and went into Roman exile again. During his mission to Hungary, he baptized St. Stephan, the future Hungarian king, and during the Roman coronation, he met with his friend from school, Emperor Otto III.

On 27 September 995, a year after Adalbert left Prague, Premyslid Boleslav II had the entire rival dynasty of Slavnik slaughtered, which only made Adalbert stay away from Bohemia. According to legend, the bishop watched the Libice massacre even though his body was in Rome. He supposedly left his glove there to prove his presence.

After that, Adalbert went through Moguntian to Poland where he and Anastase, a runaway abbot of the Břevnov Monastery, founded the Benedictine Monastery in Tremesno. In the year of 997, Adalbert and his company headed for Gdansk and farther north for pagan Pomerania. On the way there, he and his companions were killed by pagans because they supposedly desecrated a sacred grove by taking a rest there.

The Polish Prince Boleslav the Brave bought Adalbert's remains from the Prussian pagans with gold and had them buried in Gniezno. Two years after his death, Adalbert was canonized by his good friend, Pope Silvester II. The Hungarian king and Emperor Otto III made a pilgrimage to the saint's grave. An archbishopric was founded in Gniezno, and Radim, Adalbert's brother, became its first archbishop.

Adalbert returned to his homeland in 1039, when Prince Břetislav I went on a crusade to Poland and collected in Gniezno the remains of St. Adalbert, St. Radim, and the Five Holy Brothers. The saint's remains are at the Prague Castle, where later on Prince Spytihněv I founded a new basilica and consecrated it to St. Vitus, St. Wenceslas, and St. Adalbert.

The statue of St. Adalbert from the stone-cutting works of Peter Parler has been on Charles Bridge since the 14th century. The Baroque sandstone statue was created by Josef Michal Brokoff in 1709.

STATUE OF ST. VITUS

S. Vitvs.
St. Vitus

Opvs Ioan. Brokoff
Work of Jan Brokoff.

St. Vitus, one of the so-called Fourteen Holy Helpers, was born to the family of senator Hylas in Sicily in the second half of the 3rd century. Although his father was a rich pagan, young Vitus was raised by his Christian nanny, St. Crescentia, and her husband Modestus. At the age of twelve, Vitus converted to Christianity, for which his father had all three of them arrested.

They escaped from prison with the help of angels, but did not escape their fate in Lucania, Southern Italy, in 303. During Diocletian's pogrom against Christians, they and a rooster were thrown into a hot oil bath. Having miraculously survived the burning bath, Vitus, as many other Christians, was thrown to bloodthirsty lions.

But he tamed the lions, which is also shown by the statue made by Ferdinand Maxmilián Brokoff in 1714. The statue was donated to Charles Bridge by Matěj Vojtěch Macht of Löwenmacht, a dean of the Chapter of Vyšehrad.

The cult of St. Vitus became very popular. About one and a half thousand temples, churches, and shrines of this martyr were created in the entire Europe. He is especially popular in Saxony and the German Lands, where he helped to renovate the Holy Roman Empire. The veneration of St. Vitus was brought to Bohemia by St. Wenceslas, who received the saint's arm from Emperor Henry I as special appreciation. Emperor Charles IV collected other relics of the saint.

St. Vitus, made by Ferdinand Maxmilián Brokoff, is not a very good Baroque portrayal of this once much-valued martyr, the protector of the Holy Roman Empire.

STATUARY OF ST. JOHN OF MATHA, ST. FELIX OF VALOIS, AND ST. IVAN

Liberata a contagione patria coclvsa cvm Gal-
lis pace.
When the country was rid of the plague, and
peace was signed with the French.

Ioan. Franc. Ios. E. comitibvs de Thvn F. F.
Donated with joy by Jan František Josef,
Count Thun.

Opvs Ioan. Brokoff.
Work of Jan Brokoff.

Die Brückenstatuen wurden in Jahre 1854 durch Bürgermeister Dr.
Wanka restauriert.
The statues on the bridge were renovated in 1854, when Dr. Wanka
was a mayor.

The three statues, also simply called the Turk, on Charles Bridge commemorate the founders of the Order of Trinitarians, John of Matha (1160—1213) and Felix of Valois (1127—1212), who used to buy Christians captured by Turks. The center of this order was in the Cerfroid Monastery, France. The Trinitarians used to wear white habits with a hood and red-blue cross. Faithful to the legacy of their founders, it is believed that the monks bought almost a million slaves over a time period of six hundred years; however, only about thirty-one thousand have been proven. The Trinitarians spread across the entire France, Spain, Italy, and Portugal; in the 18th century, they were even in Prague, in the monastery in Spálená Street.

The statuary on Charles Bridge refers to the dreams that both saints had before they founded the order. In his dream, John of Matha saw Christians in pagan slavery and an angel with a red-blue cross on his chest that was pointing to the chained prisoners. Felix of Valois had a dream about a white stag that had an even-sided red cross between his antlers. It is no coincidence that the label of Jägermeister liquor has the same logo. It was originally made by the Trinitarians.

The kneeling figure above St. Felix is St. Ivan, a hermit that is a part of the Czech national pantheon, or let's say legends. There are several legends about him, but none of them tells us for sure when and where this mythical saint lived or where he came from.

One of the most famous stories brings Ivan to the 9th century during the rule of Prince Bořivoj. According to the legend, he settled in a cave in Český

kras in the valley of Loděnice Creek. In one of his contemplative visions, he supposedly met with John the Baptist and, with his help, chased devils out of this place. Therefore, the place where the legendary hermit lived became known as Svatý Jan pod Skalou (St. John under the Rock) and provided a refuge to Benedictine monks during the Hussite wars. Later on, a small group of Czech monks, called the Ivanites, lived there.

František Josef Thun of Klášterec ordered the statuary from F. M. Brokoff and had it adorned with his and his wife's crests. Since 1714, it has become one of the most popular statues on Charles Bridge. Nowadays the statue is rather damaged and the Charles Bridge Artists Association is renovating it.

△ The statuary from 1714, made by Ferdinand Maxmilián Brokoff, is the most famous statuary on Charles Bridge thanks to the expressive gestures of Christian prisoners and their pagan torturers. In the past, the Prague people used to scare their children with different tales about the frightening Turk walking on Charles Bridge and had the scared children count the buttons on his clothes. The statuary has deteriorated a lot over the course of time, and thus was reconstructed in 2006 from the funds collected by the Charles Bridge Artists Association operating the booths selling artwork on the bridge.

STATUARY OF THE SAVIOR, ST. COSMOS, AND ST. DAMIAN

In ista crvce nostri redemptio.
Our redemption is in this cross.

Iesv Christo Orbis medico.
To Jesus Christ, the healer of the world.

Inter divos Hippocrati Cosmae.
To Cosmos, the Hippocrates among the saints.

Pioqve fratri coeli Galeno Damiano.
To the pious brother Damian, the Galen from heaven.

Sic medicina posvit.
Thus prescribed medicine.

Hic medicina vitae.
Here is the medicine of life.

Cosmos and Damian, who lived in Asia Minor at the end of the 3rd century, are considered the patrons of pharmacists and physicians. Both men, supposedly twins, practiced the art of healing practically for free and enjoyed a great reputation. According to legend, they even performed one of the first complicated surgeries. They amputated a leg of an ill man and replaced it with the leg of a Moor, so the patient ended up with a white leg and a dark leg.

The statuary of St. Cosmos, St. Damian, and Jesus the Savior is the work of Jan Oldřich Mayer from 1709.

Both physicians probably died in Cyrrha, Syria, in 305 during the persecution of Christians by Diocletian. The prefect Lysias had them first burned, then drowned, stoned, and crucified, but in vain. They finally died by beheading.

The cult of Cosmos and Damian,[8] in whose honor Pope Felix IV had their first church erected already in the 6th century, was meant to overshadow the pre-Christian patrons of physicians, Hippocrates and Galen, which is actually obvious from the votive cartouches. Their veneration soon spread across the entire Christian Europe, and tens of churches were consecrated to these saints. Let's just mention that Czech Prince St. Wenceslas, a patron of the Czech Lands, was killed on the steps of the church consecrated to Cosmos and Damian. Emperor Charles IV also acquired a part of their remains in Bremen for the Karlstein treasure.

The sandstone statuary of both early Christian martyrs with the Savior in the middle was donated to Charles Bridge by the Prague Faculty of Medicine and made by Jan Oldřich Majer in 1709.

---

[8] The ethymology of the name of the first of the Arab brothers leads us to the word cosmos, order, and eternity. The name of Damian means hospitality and goodness.

STATUE OF ST. WENCESLAS

In memoriam festivitatis primae lustri quinti post fundationem instituti coecorum adultorum in Bohemia celebratae Pragae IV. in octob. MDCCCLVII.

In memory of celebrations of the first quarter-century since the foundation of the Institute of the Blind Youth in Bohemia that were held in Prague on 4 October 1857.

A walk past the statues on Charles Bridge can be called, without exaggeration, a walk from St. Wenceslas to St. Wenceslas. St. Wenceslas from the Grapevine Column at the corner of Crusaders Square starts the walk and the statue by Josef Kamil Böhm from 1858 brings it to an end.

Josef Kamil Böhm created several versions of the statue of St. Wenceslas for Charles Bridge in the late 1850s. Currently, on the bridge and its surroundings we can see four different statues depicting the patron of the Czech Lands. A statue of St. Wenceslas, made by sculptor Ottavio Mosto of Padua, used to be in the place of today's statue of St. Ludmila with the young Wenceslas. Its remains, pulled out of the Vltava River, are now in the Lapidarium of the National Museum at Výstaviště.

ON THE OTHER RIVERBANK

We have slowly reached the other side of the Vltava River. While walking past the statues and contemplating the life of their real models, we almost missed what other beautiful views Charles Bridge offers. We also left out several interesting things on this riverbank, about which we shall talk now.

BRUNCVÍK

Past the main river bed, there is a statue on the southern side of the first pillar built on the Kampa Island that people call Bruncvík. German-speaking inhabitants of Prague used to call it *Brunclik*. Many art historians believe that the statue of a young man in armor with a drawn sword is a statue of Knight Roland, similar to that which used to be built in France and mainly in Northern Germany as a symbol of granted city privileges. However, in the 1940s, Cyril Merhout noticed that the statue does not look like the destroyed original statue from the 15th century or the beginning of the 16th century, which was somewhat different from the typical Roland statues.

The statue of Bruncvík was placed on the bridge probably around the year of 1506. The oldest picture of the statue is in the so-called Vratislav Prospectus from 1562, and the statue is actually higher than the bridge balustrade. In the 17th century, Rudolph II had a smaller copy of the statue made from alabaster. The Swedish cannon fire at the end of the Thirty-Year War damaged the original statue, leaving behind only a fragment of the pedestal that stood there until the 19th century.

The statue called Bruncvík, which is the only statue standing on the bridge pillar on the Lessor Town bank, has undergone significant changes. While the current statue made by Šimek in the 19th century copies the traditional Roland-type protectors of city privileges with a raised sword, the original Bruncvík from the 16th century was leaning against a long, two-handed sword.

In the 1880s, the fragment of Bruncvík's pedestal was removed from the bridge and moved to the Lapidarium in Královská Obora (the Royal Game-Park). It is still there. Ludvík Šimek made a new statue according to the original in 1884. Even though he tried to be true to the original, he switched the southern and northern reliefs and created a Roland-type knight with a light sword drawn upward. According to the small copy that Rudolph had made and hardly anybody knew about because it was in Austria, the original Bruncvík was a husky knight leaning against his heavy two-handed sword jabbed into the ground.

CITY PRIVILEGES

Regardless of the new meaning given to the statue of Bruncvík, it has at least one thing in common with Roland statues. Bruncvík is a lapidified

guardian of city privileges. The statue holds the emblem of the Old Town that used to be the keeper of the bridge and both riverbanks. And as Cyril Merhout points out, the reliefs on the pedestal are also closely related to the city privileges granted by different rulers.

The reliefs on the pedestal of the original in the Lapidarium and the copy on the bridge do not have any inscription. It is possible that they used to have excerpts from, or names or issue dates of, the most important city privileges. Still, we can at least guess which document each relief pertains to.

The actual statue of the knight holding a sword in his hand and facing the bridge was supposed to watch

The symbology of the pedestal of the statue was also changed in the 19th century during the reconstruction of the statue of Bruncvík that was destroyed during the Thirty-Year War. The original pedestal is in the Lapidarium at Výstaviště.

over peace and customs duty that the Old Town started collecting on the bridge in 1435. After the Hussite wars, the younger son of Charles IV, Emperor Sigismund, decided to have the Old Town take over the Crusaders hospital, including its duty as the keeper of the bridge. The sword, as a symbol of customs clerks, can be still seen on many different emblems. In the Middle Ages, there were usually no customs duty points at the border; however, in Bohemia there was a regulation that every merchant bringing merchandise to Bohemia had to go through Prague and pay a customs duty at Charles Bridge.

The northern relief depicts a man reprimanding two children. This could refer to the privilege granted by John of Luxembourg in 1330 which says, among others, that Old Town councilors have the right to punish young men who lead a scandalous life as well as those who lend money to children without the consent of their parents. The soldier with a helmet and sword most likely refers to the privilege that pertains to the knightly status of Old Town burgesses during time of war, granted by Friedrich III in 1477. For their prior merits, Friedrich III not only added the golden walls to the city emblem, but also ordered that any Old Town burgess taken as a prisoner of war must be treated as a nobleman.

The other two reliefs are not that specific. The burgess on the southern relief could perhaps refer to the privilege regarding the bridge toll, granted by George of Poděbrady in 1459. The angel with spread wings on the western relief could symbolize the charter of Vladislav Jagellon from 1472 confirming all so-far granted privileges.

HERALDIC LEGEND

The whole of the land rejoiced when he brought the lion. And what hard work that was. The queen in particular was delighted and ordered to have the news announced to all cities, to write lion on the gates, and to place the silver lion on a red field on the land banner.

The Legend of Bruncvík,
Baworow Collection, 1472

The symbol of the Czech Lands with a two-tailed lion became the model for the first post-Habsburg state symbol stylized by Jaroslav Kursa and established on 19 May 1919.

The lion laying by Bruncvík's feet refers to the heraldic legend of Bruncvík. There exist several variants of this legend everywhere in Europe; however, in Bohemia it holds one of the most prominent positions since it shows how the heraldic lion replaced the heraldic female eagle in the Czech Lands.

The first legend of Bruncvík and his father Stylfryd appeared in the Czech Lands sometime around the year of 1400. The oldest existing written version comes from the Baworow Collection from 1472. It says that Prince Stylfryd was not happy to have a caldron as the symbol of his country. Therefore, he won the symbol of the female eagle for his country on battlefields. Later on, his son Bruncvík set out to seek adventure around the world and, after many peripeties, acquired the symbol of the lion for his country.

Bruncvík promised his wife Neomenia to return in seven years. He took to the sea in a large ship that shipwrecked later on in an unknown land. There, he fought different legendary animals. First, disguised in horse skin,

The drawing from the Sadler Prospectus (1606) was made by Filip van der Bossch and Jan Wechter. Back then, the bridge was adorned only with a huge cross.

he killed the baby birds of a large carnivorous bird with his sword, then he watched a lion fighting a seven-headed dragon. He entered into the fray on the side of the lion. The grateful lion then accompanied Bruncvík on his distressful life journey, during which Bruncvík found a magic sword that could chop people's heads off all on its own. After a long time and with the help of a sorcerer, Bruncvík and the lion finally returned home just when his wife was about to marry Prince Cleophas of Assyria. Bruncvík snuck a ring into his wife's goblet of wine to let her know that he has returned. Then he killed his rival in love. According to the Baworow Collection, Bruncvík lived to be forty-five years old and had a son called Ladislav. The lion never left Bruncvík's side, and after Bruncvík passed away the lion died of a broken heart.

Let's just add that, according to Dalimil's Chronicle, it was Prince Vladislav II who obtained the silver lion from Emperor Friedrich I Barbarossa in 1158 for his help in the crusade against Milan and thus replaced the St. Wenceslas female eagle. The lion was supposedly used only as the symbol of the Premyslid dynasty while the St. Wenceslas female eagle remained the state symbol. Premysl Ottokar I was still using the female eagle as his principal seal in 1192. As a Moravian margrave, Premysl Ottokar II obtained

Currently, the so-called great Czech state symbol uses both the Czech heraldic lion and the Moravian and Silesian heraldic female eagle.

another tail for his silver lion on a red field, and after his accession to the Czech throne in 1253, the two symbols were automatically switched. Since then, the two-tailed lion has been considered the royal symbol and the St. Wenceslas female eagle the symbol of the Premyslids.

BRUNCVÍK'S SWORD

In addition to the heraldic contents of Bruncvík's legend, we must also appreciate its alchemistic value, i.e. the traditional description of a hero's journey and encounter with many strange animals from the alchemistic list of beasts. There is also another legend regarding Charles Bridge and Bruncvík that says that Bruncvík's magical sword is hidden inside the bridge.

According to yet another legend, this magical sword that chops off the heads of all enemies all by itself belongs to Prince St. Wenceslas, who is resting with his sleeping warriors inside Mount Blaník several tens of kilometers southeast of Prague. One day, when the Czech Lands are at their lowest point and the Býkovice Pond turns red with the blood of Czech soldiers fallen in battle, Mount Blaník will break in two and St. Wenceslas, leading his army, will come out to help Prague. On Charles Bridge, he will pull his magical sword out of the stone and swing it over his head, chopping off the heads of all enemies.

Some remains of an old medieval sword were actually found under the bridge deck during the repairs of the bridge at the end of the 19th century. If, by any chance, an awakened St. Wenceslas wanted to find his sword nowadays, he would not have to pull it out of the stone, unlike the mythical Excalibur in the legends about King Arthur. All he would have to do is climb the stairway of the Lesser Town Bridge Tower, where it is usually exhibited.

STAIRWAY TO KAMPA

The Old Town had the ownership right to the Stone Bridge and both river-banks from the very beginning. However, throughout the centuries there were many changes in the ownership and consequent disputes regarding the territory adjacent to the Lesser Town fortification and the left bank of the Vltava River. The so-called Lower Island, officially called Kampa starting in 1770, was one of such territories.

Based on historical rights, the land on the Kampa Island was owned by the Old Town. However, the homeowners living on the island often considered themselves residents of the Lessor Town; they registered there and submitted to the Lessor Town jurisdiction. To make things even more

---

◁ The stairway from Kampa to Charles Bridge was built at the end of the 18th century to protect the people living on Kampa from sudden Vltava floods. Records show that mainly Prague freemasons helped with the damage caused to Kampa by the flood.

complicated, the Order of Maltese Knights, claiming its ownership right to Kampa because its seat and premises adjoined Judith's Bridge since 1169, often joined in these ownership disputes. And since the premises were located outside the Lessor Town fortification and were protected from hostile attacks only by a chain, the church of Maltese Knights has been called the Church of Our Lady "Beneath the Chain" to this day.

During the big flood at the end of the 18th century, many people living on Kampa died. To save their lives, people were climbing ladders to get to Charles Bridge, which provided a refuge. However, many of them did not make it. Therefore, in the year of 1784 it was decided to build a stairway connecting the island with the bridge.

CHAPEL OF THE HOLY BODY

The reformations of Emperor Joseph II from the 1780s considerably stirred up the Church situation in the Czech Lands. The emperor decided to close many monasteries, churches, and other religious facilities. One of the most mysterious Gothic edifices in Prague — the Chapel of the Holy Body and the Blood of Christ at Charles Square — was also a victim of these reformations. According to some sources, the rubble of the chapel was used to build the first, single-sided stairway from the Kampa Island to Charles Bridge.

If this is true, how amazing then that the pieces of the chapel that had been built by the mysterious Prague fraternity, the Circle and Hammer, ended up next to the bridge built by Peter Parler. This strange construction guild, the Latin founding deed of which still exists, was founded in the monastery Na Zderaze on 1 April 1382. It is known as the first occult fraternity that, under certain conditions, accepted even regular yet rich burgesses. Czech freemasons derive their origin from this oldest fraternity.

"The Fraternity of the Holy Body with the Sign of a Circle and Hammer in the Middle" was founded by forty people; some of them were rich burgesses, noblemen, and Church dignitaries. One of the founding members was also the grand master of the Order of Crusaders with the symbol of a red star, i.e. the order that was the keeper of the Prague Stone Bridge. According to the founding deed, three captains elected each year presided over the fraternity. One of the first captains was Peter Parler, the builder of the bridge.

The official objective of the fraternity was to build a stone chapel that would replace the wooden one standing in the middle of today's Charles

The Chapel of the Holy Body dominated today's Charles Square from the 15th century to the end of the 18th century. The ruins of this esoteric Gothic edifice are believed to have been used to build the stairway to Charles Bridge.

Square since the foundation of the square by Charles IV. The special status of this chapel was not only in its special esoteric location on the Temple Mount of the Jerusalem plan that Charles IV imprinted in the street layout of the Prague New Town, but also in the fact that the emperor had the most sacred imperial relics, such as the Holy Spear and the remains of different saints, exhibited in the chapel every year. Every Easter, pilgrims from the entire empire came to Prague, and Prague, of course, benefited from it.

In the year of 1397, Pope Boniface issued the Chapel of the Holy Body in Prague a special bull designated for the king, the captains, and fellow members that confirmed its special status. This indicates that King Wenceslas IV himself was involved in the fraternity at least as its protector even though it is quite possible that he was its secret grand master.

The chapel had a very unique octagonal floor plan resembling former commendams of the Knights Templars and the mosque Al-Aqsa in Jerusalem, where the Knights Templars founded their order. In the year of 1403, the fraternity handed the keeping of the chapel over to the Prague University, and it was Czech Church reformer John Hus who accepted it on behalf of the university. After John Hus had been burnt at the stake by the Council of Constance in July 1415, Wenceslas IV, who sympathized with his ideas, allowed lay people to practice dual communion, i.e. to take the body (bread) and blood (wine) of the Lord, which very much upset the papal curia.

Because of the dual communion practiced by many followers of John Hus, Bohemia was put under a papal interdict after the death of Wenceslas IV. During the years of 1420—1431, five crusades, known as the Hussite wars, were declared against Utraquist Bohemia.

After the defeat of the radical Hussites, the victorious King and Emperor Sigismund of Luxembourg did not impose any blood-shedding terror. The religious situation under this very skilful and intelligent ruler, who has not yet been appreciated enough by Czech history, stabilized into a rather tolerant co-existence of Roman orthodoxy and Czech moderate reformation. Reformation supporters were still rather favored in the Chapel of the Holy Body. Priest Thomas, a runaway monk of the Augustinian Order, sent to Prague by Martin Luther, the father of German reformation, started preaching in the chapel in 1524. In the 17th century, the chapel provided a refuge to the Calvinists fleeing from Germany. The anti-reformation of the Habsburgs after the Battle of White Mountain brought all this to an end by putting the Jesuits, who founded a Jesuit college near the chapel, in charge of the university and the chapel. The chapel was finally closed by Joseph II in 1784.

THE STATUARY BY MATYÁŠ BRAUN

The strange destiny of this esoteric chapel is not just in the fact that two edifices built by Peter Parler became one. The place where it happened seems to have been predestined as well.

Since, by the decision of a secular ruler, the original chapel could no longer serve as a temple of the Holy Body and the Blood of Christ, it was at least transformed into the stairway leading to the bridge exactly in the place where the blind Cistercian Luitgarda has been kissing the bleeding wounds of the crucified Christ since 1710. The mystic masterpiece sculptured by Matyáš Braun, the protégé of Count Špork who is believed to be the first Czech freemason of the 18th century, thus created a mythical entirety with the destroyed work of the founders of pre-freemasonic occult traditions in Bohemia less than one hundred years later on.

The statue of St. Luitgarda could thus be seen as a predestined memorial to the Gothic chapel, in which the actual relics related to the martyrdom of Jesus at Golgotha used to be exhibited for so many years. Occultists know that there is practically no coincidence in the spiritual world. It has also been documented that one of the first charities of Czech freemasons was the assistance provided after the flood in 1784. If the story about the rubble used to build the stairway between Charles Bridge and the Kampa Island is not true, it is at least a very clever esoteric legend. The design of the stairway as we know it today is a result of the reconstruction in 1844.

· III ·

THE BRIDGE
BETWEEN THE
WORLDS

*It is pleasure to yield to inspired frenzy, it is my pleasure to taunt
mortal men with the candid acknowledgment that I am stealing the
golden vessels of the Egyptians to build a tabernacle to my God from
them, far far away from the boundaries of Egypt. If you forgive me,
I shall rejoice; if you are enraged with me, I shall bear it. See, I cast the
die, and I write the book. Whether it is to be read by the people of the
present or of the future makes no difference: let it await its reader
for a hundred years, if God himself has stood ready
for six thousand years for one to study him.*

Johannes Kepler

A GATE TO THE COSMOS

Astronomer and historian Zdeněk Horský started deciphering in detail the cosmological symbology of the eastern façade of the Old Town Bridge Tower in the late 1970s. In his 1979 collection, One-Hundred-Year-Old Prague, he mentioned in particular the numerical symbology clearly indicating that one of the secret plans of the builders of the tower was to show, on Charles IV's triumphal arch, the entire cosmos witnessing the victory of his royal program — a union of the initiated secular reign and the ecclesiastic reign amidst the overall harmony of the cosmos.

Contrary to his predecessors, Zdeněk Horský divided the façade of the tower into four stories separated by visible ledges and attributed each story and its sculptural symbology to one of the cosmological spheres: terrestrial, lunar, solar, and celestial. It is not a coincidence to find a similar fourfold division on other buildings made by the stone-cutting works of Peter Parler, as we have already seen in the book The Prague Horologe.

COSMIC CYCLES

The Old Town Bridge Tower shows, as does the little bit younger Old Town Horologe, the cosmic cycles the way astronomers and astrologists have always known them. The author of the sculptural adornment does not use any complicated mechanical horologe device, but plays with the numbers of seemingly banal and insignificant sculptural elements on the façade instead.

Medieval cosmology saw the Earth as a fixed center of the cosmos, therefore the terrestrial sphere on the tower shows no cycles. However, in the lunar sphere above, the number of crabs

Czech historian and astronomer Zdeněk Horský (1929—1988) engaged in archeo-astronomical research and the history of astronomy. He was the first to explain the cosmological symbology of the Old Town Bridge Tower and systematically studied the astronomy of Copernicus and Kepler. He described the history of the Prague Horologe in detail. Later on, his findings were further elaborated on by others scholars.

adorning the lanceted arch of the gate clearly refers to the cycles of the Moon. There are two times fourteen crabs, i.e. a total of twenty-eight crabs, as there are twenty-eight days in a lunar month. However, astronomer Zdeněk Horský points out that the flowers are also a part of the adornment, which brings the number of days to twenty-nine and a half, i.e. the actual time of the synodic orbit of the Moon around the Earth, and offers the quote of Master Klaret from the court of Charles IV: *"Percurrit circulum vigniti luna diebus septensique simul, bis quatuor insuper horis,"* proving the back-then knowledge of syderic and synodic months.

It is the same in the higher solar sphere. The crabs on the sloping ledge above the heads of the Czech rulers stand for the day cycle of the Sun in the sky. But, contrary to the lunar sphere, the column at the top is not a part of the floral adornment, and thus a day is divided exactly into two times twelve hours and a year into twelve months.

The symbology in the fourth, celestial, sphere is more difficult to identify. However, according to Zdeněk Horský, the three times eight stars in the traceries represent the number of hours in a stellar day. The entire stellar sky appears above the Earth once in twenty-four hours. The fact that these hours are different from solar hours is indicated by the different type of adornment explaining the symbology.

As we have suggested, the statues of the saints on the façade fit the symbological interpretation of each sphere. The two Czech patrons, Sigismund and Adalbert, belong to the celestial sphere of eternity. Emperors and kings have been traditionally connected with the Sun and so is St. Vitus — Svantvitus, Apollo — standing between them. St. Wenceslas, now removed from the façade, was sometimes portrayed on a crescent moon in the Middle Ages. His title (in some languages directly referring to the Moon) entitles him to be a part of the lunar sphere of the tower as well.

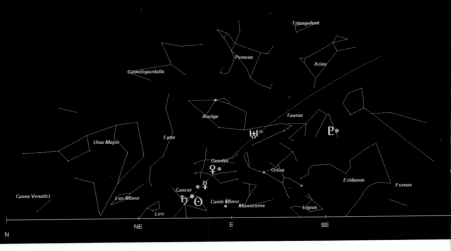

ASTROLOGICAL SIGNS

In his book Praga Mysteriosa, astrologist Milan Špůrek uses the cosmological study of Horský and takes it even further by dividing the tower by the four elements — earth, water, air, and fire — into four stories exactly at the borderlines set by Zdeněk Horský. Milan Špůrek then assigns each statue with a zodiac sign and an element according to astrology. Based on their natal charts, both Luxembourg kings were born under air signs. Charles IV has the air sign Gemini in the ascendant of his radix and Wenceslas IV has the air sign Libra. The remaining statues are assigned to different elements only based on astrological theory and practice. The fire sign Sagittarius is represented here by the ecclesiastic power of Bishop Adalbert and the fire sign Aries by the secular power of King Sigismund of Burgundy. The earth signs Virgo and Capricorn, in small reliefs on both sides of the gate, can be interpreted in a similar way. The non-heraldic lion (Leo) is rightly part of the fire sphere.

The latest astrological interpretation of the symbology includes additional numerical data completing the cosmological numbers provided by Zdeněk Horský. The data is again interpreted based on the elements in all four spheres. Thus there are twenty-eight lunar houses and two lunar nodes (wreaths with kingfishers) in the lunar sphere and three decans of each zodiac sign, the quadruplicities and triplicities of astrological aspects, and eighty-four planetary hours in a week (the number of crabs) in the solar sphere. Below the feet of the central group of statues, there are seven masks symbolizing the back-then known seven astrologically significant orbs. In the celestial sphere, the number of tracery petals indicates the back-then known forty-eight constellations as well as seventy-two years during which the constellations of the zodiac shift westward by one degree.

THE MAGIC DATE

The emperor and the master builder chose to found the bridge on 9 July 1357, a date so magic that it has been fascinating many of us to this day. If we write the date in the back-then way, i.e. 1357, 9, 7, we will get an incomplete sequence of odd numbers from one to nine and back. If we add the time, i.e. 5 o'clock and 31 minutes, the mystery is complete: 135797531.

Numerical sequences that can be read the same in both directions were very popular among occultists and given a magic meaning. Their alphabetical equivalents, the so-called palindromes, protected many Gothic edifices from evil spirits. The Old Town Bridge Tower also had such palindromes; however, the very first one was the actual date of its foundation.

While the foundation date of the bridge is historically documented, the exact time is still a mere hypothesis, in support of which historian and astronomer Zdeněk Horský put together a lot of evidence in the 1970s.

First, he proved that this way of writing dates and the time was very well known and used at the royal court of Charles IV. However, the fact that time was measured in several different ways in the Middle Ages poses a problem. Sometimes it was measured the Babylonian way, i.e. a day between sunrise and sunset was divided into equal parts (Babylonian hours) that changed throughout the year — they were longer in the summer and shorter in the winter. It was also common to measure the hours of a new day by dividing it into 24 parts starting at sunset. But none of these methods fit the assumed time of the foundation of the bridge. Thus the German way of time measuring, which was also known at the court of Charles IV, was chosen as the most probable option. The time was set in local time, as it is done today, by counting starting at midnight.

There were several good reasons for choosing this method. At that time, all back-then known (as well as unknown) astrological planets were over the Prague horizon; Mars was just rising. The constellation Lion, the regal sign always connected with Prague, was in the ascendant at that moment. Saturn was in conjunction with the Sun, which medieval astrologers considered the luckiest day of the year. And what's more, 5 o'clock 31 minutes in this system was actually morning. The Sun came out shortly after 4 o'clock, which was Charles IV's favorite time for engaging in political acts.

Stars over Prague on 9 July 1357 at 5:31 a.m. The horizon is outlined by six constellations known to astrologists from the stellar catalog Almagest of the Antique astrologist of the 2nd century, Claudius Ptolemaeus.

THE STELLAR MAP

In order to confirm his hypothesis, the meticulous Zdeněk Horský put together a large number of arguments, and thus the exact date that he had determined was then used by many other authors as well as by us since the proof of his precise thinking has been carved on the tower by Peter Parler's stone-masons for us to see.

Two adornments of the interior consoles on the eastern façade provide the key to this statement. On the left, there is a statue of a lion ripping apart a *fish tail* or perhaps a *leg*. On the right, there is an *eagle* holding a *rabbit* in his claws. If we look at the Prague stellar map on 9 July 1357 at 5:31 a.m. local time (which is about 4:33 a.m. universal time), we can see the constellation *Lion (Leo)* rising in the northeast and the last stars of the constellation *Capricorn (Capricornus)*, traditionally portrayed as half goat and half fish, the tail or leg of which the lion just caught, setting in the southwest. The *Rabbit (Lepus)* in the southeast is trying to escape from the flying-away *Eagle (Aquila)* in the west.

Are you still in doubt that the stone-masons actually carved these four points shown on the Prague horizon at the moment of the foundation of the tower? When looking at the tower, let's raise our eyes to the apex stone of the passage vault. The *crown* placed there

The constellations, shown in the sky at the moment when Charles Bridge was founded, are also reflected in console reliefs on the tower, the crown in the middle of the passage vault, and the Vltava River itself.

provides another orientation point. The *Northern Crown (Corona Borealis)* was descending over the northern horizon at that moment. On the other side of the sky, we can find the long constellation *Eridanus*. Its name is derived from the mythical river in which Phaethon drowned after his disastrous attempt to drive the Chariot of the Sun of his father, the sun god Helios. In this constellation, the Egyptians used to see the image of their sacred Nile River, and it is obvious where to look for the river here.

The stellar map was thus marked out. If the bridge had been founded just one hour later, the situation in the sky would have been different. To capture a certain moment rather exactly is nothing unusual in esoteric art.

THE MYSTERY OF CONSOLE RELIEFS

The special position of the constellations in the Prague southern sky at *midnight* on 14 May 1316, i.e. the date of birth of Charles IV, noticed by Milan Špůrek is also worth mentioning. According to him, the position of the *Lion (Leo)*, the *Eagle (Aquila)*, and the culminating *Northern Crown (Corona Borealis)* corresponds with the sculptured lion and eagle on the eastern façade and with the St. Wenceslas crown at the top of the passage vault.

The mentioned midnight, even though Charles IV was born in the morning, as well as the symbols already interpreted more accurately by a similar method, should be a warning for every careful researcher. It could be the so-called *occult veil*. This popular hermetical game is based on the principle that behind provided, somewhat misleading information, there is something more important and accurate. Moreover, the experienced astrologist indirectly challenges readers to find the position of the constellations in the sky by themselves.

Thus, if we know how to do it, we should have no problem accepting the challenge and

During the long-planned imperial coronation in Rome on 5 April 1355 at 11:00 a.m. local time, the Prague and Roman horizons showed the constellations of the Lion, Little Dog, Serpent, Eagle, Northern Crown, and Eridanus.

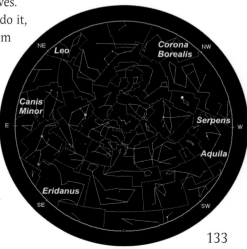

The console reliefs on the Old Town Bridge Tower also capture the moment of Charles IV's life triumph.

trying to lift the occult veil to see whether there is some other, more accurate information. We can also see the lion and eagle symbolizing the birth of Charles IV on the consoles of the western façade — the *lion* is fighting a *snake* on one side and the *eagle* is fighting a *canine* on the other side.

If we use our method of opposing constellations on the horizon depicted by console reliefs, we can in fact identify the rising *Lion (Leo)* and the setting *Serpent (Serpens)* at one moment on 14 May 1316. The second pair is then the setting *Eagle (Aquila)* and the rising *Little Dog (Canis Minor)*. The *Northern Crown (Corona Borealis)* and the *Eridanus* River are also in opposition near the horizon.

The problem with this speculation is that this moment occurred on 14 May 1316 at 7:30 a.m. The chronicles of that time say that Charles IV was born *"in the first morning hour,"* i.e. around five o'clock local time. However, the difference of two and a half hours considerably changes the entire stellar constellation, and the use of any other alternative method of medieval time measuring will not help either. Does it mean, then, that the chronicles, as well as all astrologists using this information, were wrong? Did the astrologists, usually so accurate, make a mistake in calculating the position of the constellations? Or do the symbols immortalized on the western façade relate to a different significant moment?

TWO CORONATIONS

If we check all the important dates in Charles IV's life, we shall find another date with a similar, yet even more distinct, situation in the sky with the *Big*

The console reliefs on the eastern façade were always considered moralizing scenes. Our interpretation gives them their true names: Orion and Virgo, and Hecules and Andromeda.

Dog (Canis Major) instead of the *Little Dog*. It happened on Easter Sunday, 5 April 1355, one hour before noon, i.e. exactly at the moment when Cardinal Pierre de Colombiers placed the imperial crown on the head of Charles of Luxembourg at St. Peter's Cathedral in Rome. The position of the constellations over Prague and Rome was pretty much the same. The emperor's young wife, Anne of Swidnica, whose portrayal most likely was on the western façade of the tower, was present at the coronation.

Since our method has already worked twice, why not try it a third time? Let the crown, so mysteriously connected with the Roman coronation, be our apex stone between the eastern and western walls. However, this crown resembles the St. Wenceslas crown — the crown of Czech kings that Charles IV received during a two-day ceremony, on 1 and 2 September 1347 — rather than the imperial crown.

If we check the Prague horizon at the time of the coronation of Charles IV, i.e. on 2 September about four and a half hours after sunrise, we shall find out that the constellations *Maiden (Virgo)* and *Hercules* were rising and the constellations *Andromeda* and *Orion* were setting. Let's also mention that the *Northern Crown (Corona Borealis)* and the *Eridanus* River creating the common central line of all our symbols are again near the horizon, which is no sur-

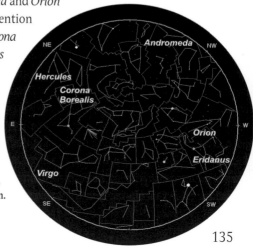

Charles IV was crowned the Czech king on 2 September 1347, probably after 10:00 a.m.

prise at all. We can now easily match the constellations Virgo and Orion as well as Hercules and Andromeda with the console adornment on the eastern façade of the tower.

Thus, the so-far more or less nameless reliefs called by people the "*Soldier and Nun*" and the "*Old Man and Girl*" got their true name back after almost six and a half centuries. Art historians and Charles Bridge guides see them as mere moralizing scenes; in the past, some people even claimed that the statue of the Soldier was Martin Luther, who took advantage of a nun. If we get through the occult haze, then Truth will reveal itself in the bright light of Knowledge. Peter Parler was not a moralist, but a God-Inspired Artist with deep esoteric knowledge.

At this point, we shall not hide anything from our inquisitive readers, but leave it up to them to try a different combination of interesting symbols on Charles Bridge that are definitely worth being thoroughly explored. The lion on the original statue of Bruncvík, probably made at the stone-cutting works of Matyáš Rejsek who carried on the Parler traditions, is ripping apart a goatling. It strikingly resembles the adornment made by Peter Parler on the Old Town Bridge Tower. The symbols on Bruncvík's pedestal also have a certain astronomical and astrological message. Let's just mention that the original pedestal of this statue is in the Lapidarium of the National Museum at Výstaviště, in the same room as the original statues from the façade of the Old Town Bridge Tower that were made by Peter Parler.

GRAND HOROSCOPES

All the world which lies below has been set in order and filled with contents by the things which are placed above; for the things below have not the power to set in order the world above. The weaker mysteries must yield to the stronger, and the system of things on high is stronger than the things below.

Kare Kosmou, Hermetica

The purpose of this publication is not to conduct large astrological research, which we shall leave to experts, but since we have three relatively accurate significant historical moments, it would be a mistake not to explore at least the basic elements of the horoscopes made for these events.

The historically first date shown on the consoles of the tower is 2 September 1347 around 10:00 a.m. local time. That is the time when

Charles IV received the Czech royal crown at the Prague Castle. We can see right away the extraordinary position of the planets in the horoscope; almost all back-then known planets were above the horizon, i.e. all except for Saturn, which is in opposition to the Sun and far below the horizon. However, in medieval astrology, the planets were given very little importance after they set, and thus it seems

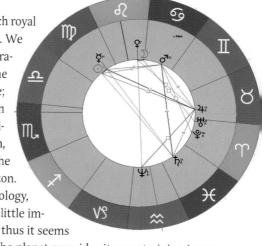

that the actual position of the planet overrides its constraining impact as well as the effects of its opposition to the Sun. And even if this is not true, certain formality, negativism, and lack of initiative of this aspect can be fought only with diligence and persistent overcoming of obstacles. These qualities are actually balanced out by the position of the ascendant in Scorpio and extremely favorable mutual aspects of Mercury, Mars, and Jupiter. Charles IV had to prove his diligence and ability to overcome obstacles since the very beginning of his reign. He raised the Czech kingdom from chaos and ruin to make it the most powerful pillar of the Holy Roman Empire, strengthened its exceptional position, and made Prague the third largest metropolis of the back-then world.

The horoscope for Charles IV's imperial coronation in Rome on 5 April 1455 at 11:00 a.m. looks even better. The grandeur of the moment is underlined in particular by rising Leo, the regal ascendant representing the energy and strong will of a true ruler. In the horoscope, we can actually see many elements typical for Charles IV's reign on the "dual throne" of the Holy Roman Empire. We should mention in particular the conjunction of Venus and Mars indicating that Charles IV's reign will not favor any extensive military operations, but skillful and elegant diplomacy. The diplomatic skills are also en-

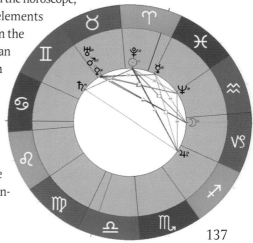

hanced by the favorable sextiles of Mercury to both these planets. Any potentially negative aspect from the horoscope of the imperial coronation is negated by the position of the Moon and Jupiter below the horizon.

The ascendant in Leo was Charles IV's favorite time, as documented by the horoscope for the foundation of Charles University (7 April 1348 after 1:00 p.m.) or the magic moment of the foundation of Charles Bridge. In both cases, all seven astrological planets were over the Prague horizon. Medieval astrologers considered the close conjunction of the Sun with Saturn, which suppresses the negative impact of Saturn, to be the best moment of the year for founding the bridge. It is interesting that the favorable trigons of Venus with the Moon and Jupiter (moreover favorably aspected by back-then unknown Neptune) indicate that the founders of the bridge endowed it with grand artistic qualities and a very harmonic foundation. When analyzing this horoscope in his book Astrological Prague, Svatopluk Svoboda, however, points out the bad position of Mercury, the unfavorable aspects of which showed up later on when the bridge was partially destroyed. Yet the position of the planets was probably so extraordinary, and the date so tempting, that the builders of the bridge were willing to take the risk.

LIONS AND EAGLES

The large number of lions and eagles adorning the Old Town Bridge Tower is too obvious to be left without any explanation. They are portrayed in the heraldic and non-heraldic way, at different levels, and in different relationships. However, their quantity and variety should not make us doubt, even just for a second, that their meaning is one of the keys to understanding the symbology of the tower, bridge, and entire city plan.

In exoteric, less mysterious interpretations, lions and eagles are explained as representatives of the Czech kingdom and the Roman Empire, or the Luxembourg and Premyslid dynasties united in Charles IV. That is surely true. It was Rudolf Chadraba who noticed the shadow cast by the

138

The shadow of the lion on the Old Town Bridge Tower touches the female eagle on the emblem below only once a year, on the summer solstice. Today, the annual mysterious scene is somewhat hindered by the net protecting the sculptures.

non-heraldic lion on the heraldic female eagle below during the summer solstice and the connection between this mystical scene and Leonine hexameters from the Roman gates. And we have just described the connection between non-heraldic lions and eagles on the consoles of the gate and the stellar sky.

The tradition to show lions and eagles together is, however, much older than the Old Town Bridge Tower and is deeply rooted. For alchemists, they signified the philosophical Sublimation of exalted mercury. Alchemist Philaletha wrote that the alchemic bringing of female eagles to a lion was one of the most difficult phases requiring ingenuity and skills and that at least seven female eagles were needed to improve the Work. So, let's count all the heraldic female eagles on the façade of the tower. There are seven of them.

ORIENTAL ROOTS

As we have already said, old astrologically inspired maps show Prague as a city under the sign of Leo, just like the entire Czech kingdom that has a lion as its symbol. Astrologers have always believed that the constellation Leo was in the ascendant of the horoscope for the foundation of the city. In the Antiquities, many cities and kingdoms were considered leonine. Some of them had ceased to exist before the history of Prague began.

A small country called Commagene, situated between Parthia and the Roman Empire, was one of the so-called leonine kingdoms. Its glory reached the highest point during the last two centuries B.C. The local religion strangely integrated the ancient Persian astrological cult of the sun god

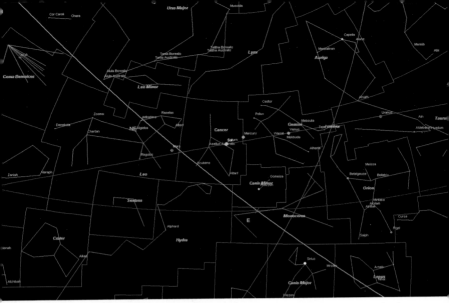

The stellar map of the sky at the moment when Charles Bridge was founded shows that it happened right before the rise of Regulus and Sirius. Such moments have had a very important meaning in astrology since the Middle Ages.

Mithras and the Hellenistic pantheon of gods. The roots of the developed Commagenian astrology go back to ancient Egyptian cults.

On Mount Nimrod in Commagene, today's Turkey, there is a mysterious monument called Hierothesion, a tumulus in the shape of a pyramid guarded by gigantic statues of gods standing on two terraces. Modern research revealed that they were actually giant horoscopes of King Antiochos Epiphanes I of Commagene for 12 July 98 B.C. and 6 July 62 B.C. Each horoscope is guarded by a lion and eagle. Both horoscopes also relate to yet another day that Commagenian astrology determined as the day for celebrating the birthday of Commagenian kings, 29 July. On that day in this region, the Sun came out in alignment with the royal star Regulus (meaning the "*Little King*"), which is Alpha Leo in the constellation *Lion (Leo)*. However, on that day in the morning, another star — Sirius from the constellation *Big Dog (Canis Major)* — came out first. Ancient Egyptians knew about the phenomenon when the bright Sirius came out before the Sun for the first time after forty days and called it the day of the birth of the new Horus, the falcon-headed sun god. These heliacal risings of Sirius marked

The reliefs of lions and eagles with a clear astrological message can be seen in the Orient as well. They are also a part of the medieval monument on Mount Nimrod in Turkey. ▷

the beginning of a new year in Ancient Egypt and always occurred during the summer solstice.

The rising of the constellation Leo with the star Regulus was thus always a very important symbol associated with the royal cult and summer solstice. Thus, it is probably not a coincidence that the constellation Leo was rising at the moment when Charles IV's triumphal arch and new bridge were founded. The ascending Leo in the sky bound the royal lion, the leonine city, and the leonine kingdom with eternity. The shadow of the lion touching the female eagle during the summer solstice symbolically captures the source of this tradition.

Thus, it is hardly a coincidence that the sloping ledge dominating the façade of the Old Town Bridge Tower looks like a Roman triumphal arch with three passages as well as a Gothic cathedral with naves built into an Egyptian pyramid in place of initiating chambers. In compliance with esoteric tradition, everything points out to one source of occult knowledge of many different civilizations. Actually, already in the 1970s Czech art historians noticed the similarity of the bizarre masks under the feet of the rulers (that the cosmological and astrological interpretation identifies with seven planets) with old Persian reliefs discovered in today's Iran.

Charles IV stressed the importance of rising Leo during the summer solstice also by another act, the meaning of which was hardly understood by his contemporaries, let alone by many future generations of historians. On 15 June 1363, Charles IV had his not quite three-year-old son Wenceslas crowned the Czech king. This act, seen as a caprice of the aging ruler who was thrilled to have an heir, was not well received in Bohemia. Archbishop Ernest of Pardubice, usually very obliging to the ruler's wishes, was also against it. Since the Coronation Rules required that kings be crowned by an archbishop, at last the emperor convinced the prelate, who has always been considered a secret professor of certain occult teachings. Thus, the new king of the Czech Kingdom was crowned in compliance with the celestial order on the day when the stellar "little king" Regulus was rising in alignment with Jupiter.

KING OF RIGHTEOUSNESS

As we know, Charles is a direct descendant of the pagan gods Saturn and Jove and of the Trojans — the son of Aeneas and Lavinia, the daughter of King John, the prince of the Etruscans and the father of Roman people — and also derives his origin from Julius Caesar from the famous Julian family. Elizabeth, the brightest star radiating both wisdom and virtues, was blessed to make a fortunate union with John, the first-born child of the great Roman Emperor Henry, out of which came a glorious son, the sunshine of the Church of God — His Majesty Emperor Charles, loved by God, strong, and having all virtues — in whom, as in a secular vessel, the two lines came together.

Jan Maringola, Kronika česká [Czech Chronicle],
second half of the 14th century

Charles IV is also portrayed as one of the Three Kings in the Chapel of the Holy Cross at the castle Karlstein, the holiest place of Charles IV's castle of the Holy Grail.

The little excursion to the Orient of long ago is not without a purpose, as it may first seem. In the year of 1353, Charles IV asked the Minorite missionary Jan Maringola, who had traveled in India, Peking, Ceylon, Babylonia, and Jerusalem at the request of the Order of Franciscans and the papal curia, to come to Prague. Charles knew him from the papal court in Avignon.

The emperor sent Maringola to a bishopric in Bisignano, Italy, and asked him to write the so-called Czech Chronicle. What he wrote is not really a chronicle in the sense according to today's historical science, but a very interesting mixture of historical events, biblical stories, and his own visions. In this spiritual chronicle, Maringola derives the origin of Charles IV from Oriental rulers-priests. In his work The Ancestry of Emperor Charles IV, Matouš Ornys names Chus of Chaldea, Nemrod of Babylonia, and Ninus of Assyria as Charles IV's ancestors.

On the other hand, the visual art of Charles IV's era associated the emperor with King Melchizedek from the Old Testament, as we can see for example in the Vyšehrad antiphonary from 1360. Melchizedek has a unique position among Old Testament figures and is often called the first priest. In the Books of Moses, Abraham — the patriarch of the Hebrews, the chosen one — recognizes Melchizedek's priesthood and supremacy over him. The Christian part of the Bible grants him the same position.

Melchizedek is king of righteousness.[9] Without father or mother or ancestral line, neither with beginning of days nor ending of life, but, resembling the Son of God, he continues to be a priest without interruption and without successor.

Hebrews 7,2—3

---

[9] = mystics (author's note)

A PASSAGE
TO THE OTHER WORLDS

I do not know any other city that would so strangely and magnificently seduce those who live there and spiritually grow together with the city, and so irresistibly invite us to visit places of its moving history, as Prague does. It seems as if the dead invite us, the living, to the places of their terrestrial existence and whisper in our ears that Prague has

Gustav Meyrink (1868—1932).

been given its name for a good reason and is, in fact, a much narrower threshold than any other place on earth...Then we walk as if under a spell, hearing and seeing nothing new that we would not already know, yet having a feeling that one can never forget — a strange feeling of having somehow crossed a threshold.

Gustav Meyrink, Neviditelná Praha [Invisible Prague], 1930

The immortal legacy carved on Gothic edifices by the stone-masons of Peter Parler makes it more and more evident that the adornment and mastership of Prague High Gothic during the reign of the initiated Luxembourgs were to manifest much deeper ideas and hidden traditions. It is beyond any doubt that none of this was happening without the knowledge of the emperor. Actually, we should rather say that the emperor himself inspired and guided the majority of it and raised his successor in the same spirit.

Based on the no longer existing group of sculptures on the western façade of the Old Town Bridge Tower, we showed that Charles IV loved to allude to his special divine predestination; however, this is not the only hint that he set before us through the symbols of the bridge.

THE KINGFISHER

Right after lions and female eagles, a kingfisher in a wreath is the most frequent symbol on the Old Town Bridge Tower. It is so typical for the tower that it is mentioned in every description of the tower. Not too many visitors to Charles Bridge pass the opportunity to count them. The message of the symbol is so simple and straightforward that we are almost embarrassed to write about it. Nevertheless, even nowadays we can sometimes read such bizarre interpretations and things that we cannot skip it.

According to Greek myths, Zeus turned the beautiful Alcyone and her husband Ceyx into kingfishers for being vain. The kingfisher fits the cosmological interpretation of the symbols on the tower by its association with solstices. Plinius says that one can see kingfishers only during solstices and the setting of the Pleiades (Alcyone is their brightest star as well as one of the stars outlining the constellation Taurus). However, the connection with the winter solstice is even better. In Antique Greece, people used to celebrate the day of Alcyone a week before the winter solstice. The celebration lasted seven days before and seven days after the solstice. It is the time when the Aegean Sea is calm and kingfishers nest. To this day, the calm weather around the winter solstice is sometimes called the "weather of Alcyone." In general, the Alcyone Days mean a joyful and peaceful time.

Balbín's complaint that people confuse kingfishers on the tower with ducks and do not know what they actually represent bespeaks that the real esoteric meaning of the symbol was hard to decipher already in the 17th century. According to Josef Svátek, people thought they were ducks even in the 19th century. The confusion could be explained by the fact that the Czech word for kingfisher (ledňáček) does not provide any direct association with the royal and spiritual power presented on the tower. However, it is not the case in other languages. The German word "*Königsfischer*" or the English word "kingfisher" gives us a clue. The kingfisher on the tower represents the Fisher King.

For a long time, people thought that the kingfisher in a wreath was actually a duck. Wenceslas IV made this esoteric symbol with a very strong meaning his personal emblem.

THE FISHER KING

You say you yearn for the Grail.
You foolish man, I am grieved to hear that.
For no man can ever win the Grail
unless he is known in heaven and
he be called by name to the Grail.

Wolfram von Eschenbach, Parzival, 468.10—14

The Fisher King is one of the central figures of the famous legend about Parzival written by Wolfram von Eschenbach in the 12th century, which is still considered one of the largest initiating medieval writings. In the legend, a gravely injured king, who cannot die until he finds his successor, is guarding the Holy Grail at his castle, a magical object providing its keeper with spiritual knowledge and material wealth.

Charles IV surely saw himself as such a Grail keeper and so did his son Wenceslas IV, who popularized the symbol of the kingfisher in a wreath with a tight node of eternal commitment. As a Grail keeper, Charles IV had the Grail Castle, Karlstein, built near Prague, where he kept the most valuable and sacred relics of the Holy Roman Empire and meditated.

When we picture the old injured Fisher King from Eschenbach's Parzival, we think of the old Emperor Charles IV, crooked and suffering from horrible gout, rather than of the young healthy Prince Wenceslas. However, so far the carved symbol of the kingfisher in a wreath is usually explained as Wenceslas IV's gratitude to Prague bath-keepers for helping him to escape from captivity, namely to the beautiful Zuzana who secretly led the king out of the Charles Bathouse and took him to the other side of the river in a boat. The alchemic meaning of this undocumented tale (the taking of the young gold-king over the stormy river) and its parallel with the legend of St. Christopher have already been revealed by Martin Stejskal in his book Praga Hermetica.

Having explained the meaning of the kingfisher on the tower, we should also elaborate on the rest of the symbol, i.e. the wreath around it. The wreath with a node is a version of the Persian bundle of rays of light that symbolized the covenant with God and the pledge of world supremacy. In the Czech language, this wreath is often called "*věník*," which relates to the expressions "*dostat věnem*" (to receive as endowment) or "*dostat do vínku*" (to be endowed). The entire symbol only enhances the same symbology of the no longer existing sculptures on the western façade — Charles kneeling in front of baby Jesus. The power entrusted by God is not only secular but also spiritual and, for the Fisher King, represents an irrevocable commitment.

THE CELESTIAL JERUSALEM

Even though Wolfram von Eschenbach speaks of the Holy Grail as a magic stone, modern scholars believe that this object of desire and quest of many knights is a certain state of soul, knowledge available to all but found only by a few. Thus, it is not an object from this world and can be found only at the borderline between the physical world and the spiritual world. And this is exactly where in Prague we find the symbol of the Grail keeper, the Fisher King.

In the book about the Prague Horologe, we talked about Charles IV's esoteric concept of the city based on the fourfold

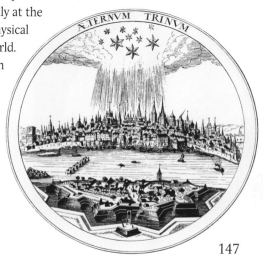

symbology of the Celestial and Terrestrial Jerusalems. The physical level of being is represented by the actual city, the New Town, the streets network of which was modeled after that of the Celestial Jerusalem as it was known to European scholars in the 14th century. The astral level is represented by the silhouette of the Prague Castle above the river. Charles IV had the castle towers, which no longer exist, gilded so that they would symbolize the Celestial Jerusalem in the Revelation of St. John.

Both these symbolic worlds in Prague can be seen from the same sacred place, the Old Town Bridge Tower. On one side of the tower, the city and its life start; on the other side, we have a view of the majestic Prague Castle.

Occult teachings say that the physical world and the astral world are connected by the etheric level. In the esoteric concept of the city, we chose the Prague emblem of the era of Charles IV to be the etheric level.

The emblem encompasses the archetypal characteristics of the Celestial Jerusalem — its silver walls correspond with the white gold walls of the city from the Apocalypse, its three towers symbolize the Holy Trinity, and its open gate made of gold suggests that anybody can enter. The gate and towers on the emblem were probably given the appearance of the Old Town Bridge Tower and the symbolic couple of Lesser Town towers in the background at the end of the 14th century, which surely was not a coincidence. The tower and the bridge are the actual link between the two worlds, the etheric gate to eternity.

THE GOTHIC ARCH

Our interpretation of the symbolic meaning of the tower and the bridge as the etheric link between the astral world and the physical world is also supported by other evidence right from the tower. Mr. Maixner's renovation of the original Gothic painting on the passage vault enhanced the rich green floral adornment. Even a less experienced seeker of me-

The Gothic lanceted arch very much resembles a mandorla, "vesica piscis," used in Christian iconography as the sign for a passage to higher worlds. We can see the esoteric meaning of this symbol in pagan symbology and in the hieroglyphic Ru with all its connotations, including sexual ones.

dieval occult symbology would not doubt that this is the etheric plane of existence as indicated by the original painter. Above the exit from the passage, we can see the face of Jesus Christ. Since the sacrament at Golgotha, the esoteric Christian tradition has considered Christ the etheric body of the Earth. He is the instrument for making the transition between the worlds.

It is rather symbolic that the gateway between the worlds leads through portals in the shape of a typical Gothic lanceted arch that strikingly resembles the Egyptian hieroglyphic *Ru*, the Christian image of which looks like a *mandorla,* also called the "fish bladder," *vesica piscis*. This special image is usually shown around Jesus Christ, the Virgin Mary, or other saints and always symbolizes a passage to another level of existence. The hieroglyphic *Ru* in arcanic art, often that of pagan and pre-Christian times, is usually mentioned in a sexual context since it resembles a vagina through which man comes into this world.

The solstice mystery of the Sun setting over the grave of St. Vitus in the Cathedral of St. Vitus on the photographs taken by Jan W. Drnek.

CANONIC ORIENTATION

We know that, when building the bridge, Peter Parler used only the western end of the original Judith's bridge leading to the streets of the Lessor Town. He moved the eastern end of the bridge and its new tower several meters to the south, visibly curving the bridge on the eastern side in order to give it an almost perfect east-western orientation. Thus, the bridge crosses the river parallel to the original bridge only a little bit more south.

Such radical changes in Prague edifices of the era of Charles IV always had a secret spiritual meaning, which is also the case of the famous annual solstice phenomenon happening right by the Old Town Bridge Tower. When standing at the foot of the Old Town Bridge Tower on the day of the summer solstice (i.e. the medieval holy day of St. Vitus, the co-patron of the bridge), we can see the Sun set above the Cathedral of St. Vitus exactly at the place where the relics of St. Vitus are kept. If we make a connection between St. Vitus and the Slavic sun god Svantvitus, we get an excellent mysterious scene worth the reputation of both our Master Builders. And the fact that this spectacle has been somewhat blocked by the statue of St. Bernard since the 18th century makes no difference.

The esoterically-oriented artist Alfons Mucha captured the mystery of the setting Sun on the summer solstice already in 1918 on one of the first stamps of free Czechoslovakia.

THE IMPACT OF THE ELEMENTS

For antique and medieval builders, a bridge traversing a wide river was always one of the most difficult undertakings. By its nature, a bridge is subjected to harsh tests, the impact of practically all known elements. A bridge must resist the enormous pressure of rushing *water*, is mercilessly hit by the *air* of blasting wind that encounters no natural obstructions above water, is exposed to the blazing heat of solar *fire* from which there is no escape, and its foundations must withstand the movements of the *earth* on which it stands.

A successful bridge builder must take all these factors into consideration. Yet there is another element, the most mysterious and the least known, called the fifth element. The mysterious *quintessence* has been described mainly by alchemists and magi since a very long time ago. Occult teachings see the quintessence as *ether*, a non-material, all-reviving, and all--penetrating substance that has nothing to do with the chemical ether. In the symbolic language of the initiates, ether was often represented by a circle with a dot to make it clear that the circle is not empty. Its similarity with the astrological symbol for the Sun is not a coincidence.

According to occultists, ether is quiescent and penetrates the entire cosmos. The Earth, slowly making one full rotation in one day, is in the etheric space. The rotation

The etheric symbology of the link between the two worlds is also obvious from the adornment in the passage of the Old Town Bridge Tower.

151

movement of our planet causes quiescent ether to seem to gently blow on its surface from the east to the west. This etheric breeze, *the Voice of God from the East*, has always been known to the mystics. It always played a very important role in religious and magical rituals as well as in architecture, in particular the floor plans of sacred edifices.

Peter Parler's canonic east-western orientation of the Prague bridge creates the least possible resistance to this faint yet powerful etheric breeze. The bridge does not change its direction until it reaches the Lessor Town bank, where it is standing firmly on the ground and is no longer exposed to water and air. The harmony with the non-material etheric current around the planet amplifies even more the secret function of the bridge as the etheric connection between terrestrial "reality" and the transcendent worlds.

HIDDEN MYSTERIES OF THE TOWER

So far we have explored the symbology of the Old Town Bridge Tower and Charles Bridge from different angles and at different levels, but only from the outside. Let's explore the inside of the tower to see what else we can find out and add to our previous discoveries. The northern and southern façades of the tower have no adornment, and if there was ever any planned, we shall not discover its secrets because it was probably never finished.

In our quest for another mystery, we must go up a spiral stairway adjoined to the southern wall, which is now open to the public. On the

We can go up the Old Town Bridge Tower on the stairway in the addition on the southern side of the tower.

first floor, we must pay a small admission fee, can watch a short film about some revealed secrets of the bridge, and see two beautiful stained glass windows with kingfishers that are not easy to spot from the street. On the second floor, we can see a nicely renovated room and get psychologically ready for new wonderful things to see.

On the way to the top of the stairway, we pass by the remains of what could have been the adornment of the southern wall before the stairway was added on and, from the narrow gallery, we can admire the beautiful panorama from this unusual angle. According to Mr. Havránek, the Latin palindrome protecting the tower from evil spirits is somewhere here. It is believed that if the palindrome is quickly read back and forth, it will scare these spirits away. Unfortunately, nowadays we can see here only a bunch of inscriptions carved in the wall by tourists.

EXPOSURE OF THE KEYHOLDER

One would have to be blind to miss the statue at the top of the spiral stairway. It is a statue of a crooked man in a long coat that people call the *Keyholder* or the *Tower Keeper*.

This life-size statue hidden inside the tower has always drawn attention of those interested in the history of the bridge and its towers since, at that time, it was absolutely uncommon to make a portrayal of a seemingly insignificant person. The statue does not represent any ruler, god, or saint to whom similar statues were usually built. It does not even have a name. Many take offence at the way the man is depicted. Yes, in a rather frivolous gesture, the crooked old man actually lifts his kilt and shows off his naked bottom to all passers-by!

Yet such portrayals are nothing unusual in arcanic art, and only those who know nothing about the meaning of this gesture consider it indecent and crazy. Only a fool, who has not noticed that this surely respectable man is in fact exposing his *most intimate secrets*, would laugh or take offence

The stone statue called the Keyholder, or the Tower Keeper, has been damaged by tourists walking by. Yet, his exposed bottom is still hard to miss.

at the naked bottom of the Keyholder. It would be more appropriate to bow before his naked truth. It is not us, but the stone *holder of the keys* to the meaning of the sculptural adornment of the tower who exposes the ancient mysteries to anyone who wants to see them.

For this reason, we very much regret that the face of the stone Tower Keeper has been partially damaged because we cannot help thinking that the face of our jovial stone brother should be compared with the bust of Peter Parler located in the triforium of the Cathedral of St. Vitus. Then the exposure of the Keyholder would probably be complete.

THE TAROT FOOL

The archetype of the fool exposing his intimate parts has been known to those engaged in the esoteric art for centuries. We can find him on traditional tarot cards, in which the Fool has a special position, as well as on many artworks of spiritual painters from different centuries. The Fool is usually a favorite topic in literature and is encoded in many sculptures of esoterically inspired architecture. It is not a coincidence that the legendary alchemist Fulcanelli dedicated important parts of his work to the symbolism of the Fool and medieval festivities inspired by the Fool.

On his journey in the pack of tarot cards, the wise Fool is permanently confronted with many more or less obvious symbols. He is not afraid to take a crucial step with a carefree smile where others see only an abyss into

which he can fall. With his knowing eyes, he can see an invisible bridge growing under his feet that he can safely cross and be on his way — on his way to the other side. Just like the Fool, our Keyholder, surrounded with stone symbols, knows that the bridge is not only made of stone as he is. Thus, to people around he can naturalistically show some of his secrets. He who understands his *exposure* will understand. He who does not understand it will see nothing but an exposed *naked bottom*.

A JOURNEY TO ETERNITY

Throughout the centuries, Charles Bridge did not witness only military conflicts described by the official positivistic history, but also those that were unyielding, less visible, spiritual, almost occult.

The triumphal arch of the Old Town Bridge Tower openly glorified Charles and his son Wenceslas as emperors — high priests, the secular and ecclesiastic heads of the world. This concept, far from the later on triumphant Roman doctrine of popes, could not go unnoticed by the Jesuits, the most zealous papal henchmen of the Baroque era.

JESUIT OPPOSITION

The complaint of Bohuslav Balbín, the Jesuit historian of the end of the 17th century, about the fact that people of his era do not even understand the true meaning of the kingfishers on the façade and confuse them with ducks, shows how much the educated Jesuits understood the hidden meaning of the symbology of the Old Town Bridge Tower that was often way beyond official Church symbols. The Society of Jesus, well aware of the

The members of the Society of Jesus played a major role in the recatholization of Bohemia at the beginning of the 17th century. Educated Jesuits were very well aware of the esoteric legacy of the Gothic adornment from the era of Charles IV in Prague and therefore founded their seats in close proximity to the most prominent monuments of the initiated emperor. Next to the Chapel of the Holy Body at Charles Square, they built a Jesuit church and large college, and right across from the Old Town Bridge Tower, they erected the Church of the Holy Savior with an army of Baroque statues and the Jesuit college Clementinum.

Ignatius of Loyola (1491−1556) was the spiritual father and co-founder of the Society of Jesus and one of the greatest Christian mystics.

magic power of the legacy of Charles IV and Wenceslas IV, moved to the nearby Clementinum, monastic premises leading to Crusaders Square right across from the Old Town Bridge Tower. They symbolically countered the concept of the tower façade, *caesar pontifex maximus*, with their concept, *ecclesia triumphans* (the Church Triumphant), on the triumphant portico of the Church of the Holy Savior built in 1653 directly across from the bridge tower. The Jesuits tried to beat the triumphant consecration of the bridge tower with the consecration to the highest "triumphant" saint: Jesus Christ, the Savior. The magic power of the figures made by Peter Parler is countered with an army of fourteen Baroque statues of saints headed by the triumphant Savior accompanied with four evangelists.

In their spiritual opposition to the medieval concept of the initiated Luxembourgs, the anti-reformation Jesuits went even further and decided to "decorate" the simple Gothic bridge with Baroque statues. They first felt uneasy about the historically questionable, thin legend about John of Nepomuk's martyr death, carried out by King Wenceslas himself after John of Nepomuk had refused to divulge the secrets of the confessional, because it could have ended up with a big embarrassment for them. However, when the Jesuits realized that in some way the statues on the magic bridge worked as a weapon against Charles IV's concept of the city, they did not hesitate to use the legend.

The statues placed on the bridge, which used to be adorned only with a simple Holy Cross, first represented only properly proven Jesuit patrons — St. Francis Xavier and of course the founder of the Society of Jesus, St. Ignatius of Loyola. However, the strict Jesuits also kept an eye on other saints that their co-religionists wanted to add to the bridge. In the year of 1714, the bridge was already adorned with twenty-six statues from the pantheon of Catholic saints who, at different times and in different ways, were opposed to what the enlightened Luxembourg emperor embodied in the esoteric concept of the bridge and its surroundings — the union of the secular reign and the ecclesiastic reign, the supremacy of the Roman emperor to the pope, and the quest for eternity through knowledge and initiation. The so-far pure jewel of esoteric Christianity was symbolically covered with blood and a thick cloud of intolerance and idolatry.

THE GERMANIC BRIDGE

The rising Jesuit *ecclesia militans* (the Church Militant), represented by the two lines of Christ's warriors carved in stone, could not go unnoticed by other religious orders, in particular the Order of Cistercians because construction was its main area of interest since its foundation. And thus these heirs of the secret of the Knights Templars, keepers of ancient esoteric knowledge, and bearers of the language of the birds, the ever-green language of the initiates, made their own sculptural contribution, the esoteric value of which far exceeds any other sculpture on the bridge.

Even back then, the army of deceased saints guarding the bridge could have evoked the Ancient Germanic mythical hall Vallhalle described in the Icelandic epos Edda written by Snorri Sturluson in the Middle Ages. In Valhalle — near the rainbow bridge Bifrost separating Asgard, the realm of the gods, from Midgard, lower spiritual spheres — slain warriors sleep, awaiting their last fight during the final Ancient Germanic apocalypse, Ragnarok. The fight will start after Bifrost is attacked by Midgard giants, which will be announced by the crowing of the bridge guardian, the gold-comb-adorned rooster Gullinkambi.

The symbology of Charles Bridge as the archetype of Bifrost, the bridge between the two worlds, is enhanced by the unique location of the statue of the founder of the Cistercian Order, St. Bernard. Yes, on the second pillar right behind the bridge tower, Gullinkambi crows from the statue of St. Bernard and announces that hostile giants attacked the bridge and are heading for Asgard! The dice by his feet suggest to those who know mathematics that his presence is not coincidental.

GABRIEL'S MESSAGE

If Gabriel wished to change his appearance, he would take your face from this statue, Bernard. On Gabriel's Ave you, the best father, will receive Salve. On our Salve, give us your Ave.
Text under the statue of St. Bernard on Charles Bridge, 1709

We can be sure that the statue of the founder of the Gothic style has a deep message that his admirers from the beginning of the 18th century tried to convey to us in a way that was appropriate for the Gothic rather than the pompous Baroque. They must have been aware of the immense tension created in Crusaders Square by the opposition of the two differently designed triumphal edifices. And we can tell from the statue of St. Bernard of Clairvaux whose side they took.

The text that Benedict Littwerig, an abbot of the monastery in Osek, had carved on the pedestal of his donation to Charles Bridge is somewhat mysterious. It addresses St. Bernard and mentions archangel Gabriel, who is not a part of the statue. It is hard to believe that it would be only because, in Church tradition, Gabriel is the herald of the immaculate conception of the Virgin Mary to whom Bernard looks up in his vision.

In order to explain this small mystery, we must go all the way to the work *De Septum Secundeis* (The Seven Secundary Intelligencies), written in 1508 by the German mystic Benedictine abbot Johannes Trithemius, who was very well known in occult circles of that time. Secundeis are seven planetary angels (archangels) who, during a certain time, rule European history in a preset order. Trithemius calculated the cycle of their reign, starting with the birth of Adam, based on biblical data and set 15 March 5202 B.C. as the beginning of their reign. Ever since then, the archangels in turn rule the world for 354 years and 4 months.

It was archangel Gabriel who, according to Trithemius's system, ruled when the statue of St. Bernard was created. And when we realize that St. Bernard's face on the bridge is exactly how the Father of the Gothic used to be portrayed and actually has *Gothic features*, then our question is almost answered. The Cistercians were convinced that leading archangel Gabriel, whose rule started around the year of 1525, would have preferred the Gothic look of St. Bernard. All this is carved in the place from which, when looking from the bridge toward the portico of the Church of the Holy Savior, one cannot miss the statue of St. Bernard.

A MAGICAL DUEL

The careful breaking and reversing of the Jesuits' elaborate magical web trying to conceal the Gothic essence of the place, the medieval way of expressing hidden ideas, and the direct reference to the European occult tradition give a new meaning to another symbol next to the rooster — the glove of a Roman soldier. Together with the rooster and dice, it reminds us of Caesar's crossing of the Rubicon after his victorious march on Rome. In a way, it is also a knight's glove symbolically thrown at the expanding Jesuits, a bold occult slap to those trying to crush and obliterate genius loci. The angels are pulling down the *vera icon*, the true image of God, and showing that the cross leaning against *the rock* is empty. Christ is in heaven, in the arms of his mother, and St. Bernard is looking up at her the same way Charles IV used to sixty years before just a few meters higher — on the tower.

It is almost a visible magical duel between the two concepts that took place at the beginning of the bridge connecting two worlds. When walking on Charles Bridge toward the Old Town, we never forget to greet the statue of St. Bernard in the Roman way: *Salve!* And in the noise of seagulls, cars, street musicians, and tourists, we can some-times almost hear someone's faint, yet almost amused: *Ave…*

THE QUEST FOR GOLD

The Church of St. Francis, built based on the design of the French architect living in Prague, J. B. Mathey, represents the oldest import of Roman churches with a dome to Central Europe. The architect was inspired by St. Peter's Cathedral in Rome and other Roman edifices when designing the façade of the church. We do not know whether the alchemic reliefs on the façade were a part of the original Gothic church, of which only the foundations are left, or come from the Baroque reconstruction in the second half of the 17th century.

In the astrological interpretation, we have identified the Vltava River under Charles Bridge with the Eridanus River that the Greek hero Iason sailed on his ship Argo during his journey to Kolkhis to retrieve the golden fleece. This comparison is not at all incidental. Where else should an Argonaut seeking gold treasure go if not to the place in Prague where the Sun — the hieroglyphic for gold — demonstrates many mysteries every year and where our mind is captured by the beauty of the solar symbology on the triumphal gate of the renowned emperor?

We must mention another mystery that makes the magical power of Crusaders Square complete. After Judith's Bridge had been built, the entrance to the bridge from the Old Town bank was guarded by the residence of the Order of Crusaders, which, together with its church, form the northern side of the square. The church and other buildings have been gradually remodeled and modernized, yet there is one place that we should not miss. It is the portal of the Church of St. Francis created by architect J. B. Mathey and master-builder D. Cannevalo in the 17th century.

We are not the only ones, and certainly not the first ones, intrigued by the hermetic charge of the statues on the portal of this old church. In spite of knowing how sacred this place is, we would like to comment on this rather unique collection of hermetic symbols in Bohemia. There is almost no doubt that the ten reliefs on the crown ledge of the portal and the other three reliefs in separate cartouches concern the ancient art of making gold pursued by scholars around the world. Prague was no exception; actually, during certain time periods, Prague was a renowned paradise for them.

TWO WAYS

According to alchemic literature, there are two ways to achieve a goal, from which one must choose ahead of time. A longer, more difficult, but far more rewarding way is called the wet way. An alchemist using this way works in his laboratory with two secret matters called mercury and sulphur, mixing and purifying them for many long days and nights in order to achieve his goal — the philosopher's stone that turns regular metals into gold or silver.

The other alchemic way to attain the philosopher's stone is called the short, or dry, way. This way is shorter and faster, yet more dangerous and difficult to control. During this method, an alchemist uses a single crucible and a single matter, mercury, for just one week. The central relief of the entire collection on the Church of St. Francis indicates the short way of making gold. The relief with a burning lamb, which was also a Christian symbol of the Eurocharist, is a common portrayal of this way.

The dry way takes a completely different direction than the wet one, which is also indicated on the first relief by the stretched sails that are pushing the vessel of the Work back against the direction of navigation. The dramatic nature of this scene, in which even waves take the direction of the blistering wind, is just a preview of what actually happens during this short alchemic process. In order to sail in such a storm, the vessel must have a very strong mast, which looks like a cross here (in alchemy, the cross is a common hieroglyphic for a crucible). If the mast were not strong enough and broke too early, the ship would wreck and the Work would be destroyed.

PRIMA MATERIA

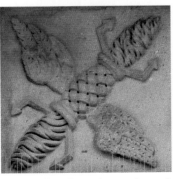

The fact that, in this case, the matter of the Work is dry, fixed, is also demonstrated by the relief with the anchor. The anchor is a device that was always used to attach, *fixate*, unstable ships to the ground. Our anchor looks like a cross resembling the letter T just like the mast — crucible — on the ship. A rope entwines the anchor similarly to the rope of the mast on the previous relief.

From the rope entwining the anchor and mast it is just one step to the next relief, on which a serpent entwines the Tau cross. This symbol is known from famous alchemic writings; for example, the great scholar Nicolas Flamel wrote about it. According to alchemists, the serpent, the ancient sign for matter, must be attached to the cross with three gold nails, similarly to what Moses did with a serpent in the desert.

But what do we know about the matter that must be handled this way? Not much. The strange flower with three petals growing from the depths of the earth, together with several strangely twisted stalks, on the next relief could give us a clue. We can find this flower in old alchemic writings. And Venus's hand mirror, in which a few alchemists found the missing pieces of the puzzle, could also have something to do with the mercury of the Work.

However, we are almost sure that this mysterious matter that many sought and few found must be treated in compliance with the rules of the Art before being alchemically processed. The dry way uses only one matter, mercury, the attribute of which has always been the caduceus that we can see on the next relief of the Church of St. Francis. Here, the caduceus consists of two lightning bolts that are strangely entwined around a central rod and point out the necessity for artistic treatment of the matter. It is not until the matter is properly purified that the typical symbol can appear, confirming the correct choice of matter. Whiffs coming out on both sides and the wings added to the symbol indicate that the mercury is free of any volatile substance, and the fixed matter is ready to go into an alchemist's crucible.

OPUS MAGNUM

A censer, another typical portrayal of a crucible used in the dry process, is easy to spot from a distance among

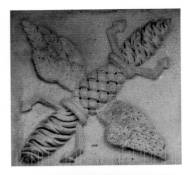

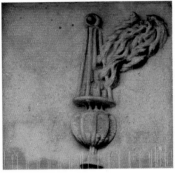

the symbols on the Church of St. Francis. When looking closely, it appears, however, even more occult because the smoke is not coming out of the censer; instead, it seems to be going in. Is this perhaps the key to the success of the entire process?

An alchemist who decided for the dry way cannot be disturbed by questions because the very next symbol is telling him that he must be as quick, direct, systematic, and accurate as a bullet pinning a heart to a tree trunk. The process with a crucible must be done under very high temperatures and cannot be tainted. Moreover, the matter must be amalgamated several times. And just as the mythical bird phoenix dies in flames and is reborn from the ashes, the success of an alchemist is born in the heat of fire and the sweat of his brow. This is shown on the next relief in which a bird is flying out of its aflame nest.

We can see the same bird on the next relief; this time it looks more like a dove with a twig in its beak, which is the symbol of hope that Noah, the patriarch of the Old Testament, saw at the end of his voyage and that the creator of the Work must nurture during the whole time. Perhaps the most mysterious relief, the one before last, indicates that if a scholar of the Royal Art carefully works in compliance with the canon of the Science, avoids all pitfalls and perils of the chosen way, and shows sufficient skills and knowledge of mysterious, yet simple operations, his crucible will break at the end. Then, he will be able to scrape small enlightened pearls of his success out of the bottom. The intoxicating grapes of happiness, the Christian symbol of the blood of Christ, will then become a well-deserved materialization of the same spirit that he sought.

The Roman emperor — Sol Invictus (the Undefeated Sun) — was thus appropriately glorified in this place. The Easter lamb is burnt, Christ — gold rose from the dark grave.

· IV ·

THE BRIDGE
TO KNOWLEDGE

We have thoroughly explored magical Charles Bridge and its surroundings. We crossed the bridge back and forth several times, looked at the monuments from the ground, water, and inside. Our journey may have provided several new small pieces to the grand mosaic of what Magical Prague actually is, where its magic comes from, and who the people partaking in its creation were. At the end, let's add several small notes to what we have seen during our journey.

THE HISTORY OF THE BRIDGE

As it usually is with old edifices, one of the first questions that come to mind is how old they are exactly. Our interpretation of the esoteric symbology of the bridge only confirms the exact date of the foundation of the bridge. The magic date, 9 July 1357, 5:31 a.m., thrilled the bridge founders with both its numerical symbology and its special position of the planets in the sky so much that they decided to immortalize it in stone.

On the other hand, when approximately the Stone Bridge finally connected both riverbanks is a more difficult question that many generations of Czech historians have been trying to answer. In this respect, our best clue will be the tale about the priest Martin Cink, who was thrown off the bridge into the river at the place where the emperor had the Calvary cross erected in commemoration of this horrid act that is believed to have happened in 1361. Thus, only four years after the construction had begun, Old Town burgesses, who carried out this merciless execution, were already able to reach the middle of the bridge. And there is nothing saying that the bridge, from which the priest was thrown off, was unfinished. But even if the bridge were not finished and completely opened by that time, it is obvious that the historians estimating that the bridge was not finished until the end of the 1370s or even later must be wrong since Peter Parler's stone-masons were known for working very fast. Since Judith's Bridge was built just in three years, it should not have been a problem to build this very important transportation route as fast several hundred years later on.

Art historians are not sure when the sculptural adornment on the Old Town Bridge Tower was created either. Was it during the rule of Charles IV or Wenceslas IV? After having examined many hidden meanings of the

The interpretation of the symbology of the Old Town Bridge Tower indicates that the sculptural adornment was designed during the rule of Charles IV and probably completed after his death. ▷

entire artistic design of the façade of the tower, we can easily say that the basic concept was realized during the life of Charles IV. The emblems of the lands clearly indicate that the adornment was carved toward the end of Charles IV's rule since his successor, Wenceslas IV, lost some of them shortly after. The entire esoteric concept also more or less glorifies the rule of Charles IV and his lifelong concept of the union of the secular reign and the ecclesiastic reign on the "dual throne" of the Holy Roman Empire and records important events from his life. Thus, it is very likely that both the design and the position of the basic adornment elements, ledges, crabs, small sculptures, and emblems of the lands on the eastern façade come from the era of Charles IV.

It is possible that the adornment on the western façade of the tower, which has been destroyed, was also completed during his life. However, the large statues on the eastern façade — the statues of both emperors and saints — were probably not created during Charles IV's lifetime. We arrive to this conclusion based on the fact that the look of the young King Wenceslas corresponds rather with what he looked like after the death of his father and that the central statue of St. Vitus, in the pose of the Roman victorious Apollo, resembles the canon of the Church of St. Apollinaris in Prague, Václav of Radeč, who did not become a canon until the 1380s.

The famous kingfishers are another unresolved mystery. Were they placed on the Old Town Bridge Tower during the rule of Charles IV or Wenceslas IV? Either is possible. It is true that it was Wenceslas IV who made the kingfisher in a wreath famous and later on made it his personal emblem, yet there are still some doubts. The Grail symbology of the Fisher King points to the old injured initiated king rather than the young, healthy, happy, and prodigal prince who, in spite of his Grail upbringing, suffered his "injuries" in difficult "battles" of his life much later on.

The copper engraving of Václav Hollar from 1636 shows that the Stone Bridge in Prague was practically without any statues until the second half of the 17th century. There was only the statue of Calvary in the place from which the priest Cink was thrown into the river in 1361.

EMPEROR — HIGH PRIEST

Charles Bridge, as well as the entire Prague rebuilt by Charles IV of Luxembourg, who has been recently voted by people as the greatest Czech in history, say a lot about his personality. The incredible charisma that still radiates from his legacy puts him way above any secular ruler and spiritual authority who has ever had power in this part of the world.

The genetic dispositions of the two prominent European noble dynasties made a fortunate union in Charles IV. From his mother Elizabeth's side, he was a descendant of the ancient prominent Premyslid dynasty that, during many centuries of its rule, achieved a sovereign position in a somewhat wild part of Europe and gained the respect of all European monarchs. Premyslid princes and kings became successful not only on battlefields, but also in spiritual fields. From his father, John of Luxembourg, he inherited all positive qualities of a true medieval knight as well as a direct kinship with renowned royal dynasties of the western, more civilized, part of Europe. This gave him a great start to becoming a successful ruler later on.

Charles IV's childhood, the least known part of his life, surely played an important role in his life. As a four-year old boy, he was violently separated from his mother by his father and confined in seclusion at the castle Loket. He spent two months in a dark castle basement with hardly any light and a year in isolation at the castle. None of the existing documents mention how much all this affected the little boy's mind, and Charles never talked about it. Recently, many studies have been done on a long-time stay in the dark, showing that many mystics and mystical esoteric rites used this method to initiate the astral abilities of the human body. Actually, a long-time stay in the dark is used abroad to treat certain psychological

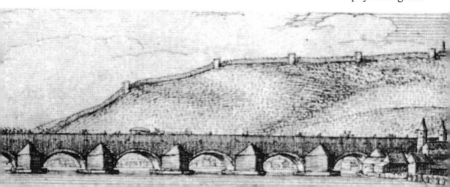

problems, e.g. German esoteric Holger Kalweit, who is well known in our country, has been successfully practicing so-called dark world therapy. Charles IV's mystical experiences, visions, clairvoyant "dreams," and "miracles," as well as inclination to monastic meditating in seclusion, indicate that we may not be far from the truth.

After the shocking experience from his early childhood, Charles IV was suddenly thrown into a completely different world. When he was eight years old, his father sent him to his relatives at the French court so that the young prince could receive a proper education. As Charles IV says later on in his own biography, he was well received in France, was given a lot of love, and had great teachers. Was it perhaps the initiation by separation and the dark as well as the inherited dispositions that made the young man absorb, like a sponge, all the new information and stimuli received at the French court, which then became an integral part of his personality for the rest of his life?

Charles IV's education did not involve only the study of languages and the bigoted Catholic interpretation of Christianity, as it could first seem. Even though theologian Pierre Roger, later Pope Climent VI, was his most famous and probably also most beloved teacher, he was not the only one. Charles IV's deep knowledge of pre-Christian European and Oriental mythologies, frequent use of astrology in regular life and political acts in particular, deep understanding of the magical effect of sacred relics and diligent pursuit of collecting them, as well as extraordinary talent for collaborating with the most competent esoteric figures of that time indicate that he had to be also *initiated* in the knowledge that was at, and often beyond, the borderline of the usually provided education.

The small examples of how the emperor used astrology in practice that we provided here clearly show that the horoscopes of his major political acts reflect in particular those things that he sought and later on fulfilled in practice. Therefore, Charles IV and his advisors had to plan and carefully calculate them ahead of time. The major focus on the favorable position of the planets and the stellar sky above when making important political decisions must thus be seen as the main reason for postponing (sometimes even for many years) or precipitating many of his political deeds. However, today's positivistic history is not able to understand the strange behavior of the initiated emperor and often looks for different obscure explanations

that have nothing to do with the reality of the era of Charles IV. It seems that if Charles IV did not behave this way, today's historians would have nothing to speculate on since many things would not have been materialized or would have failed just like in the case of many other rulers who did not follow the ancient celestial principles.

Charles IV's concept of the emperor — high priest on the "dual" throne of the Holy Roman Empire and affirmation of the imperial authority in the spiritual area even against the pope's interests were successful only during his rule. The fact that he was able to affirm this concept through his clever politics is rather unique in European history. Many much more famous and noted emperors had tried more or less successfully to put similar pressure on the papacy before, but lacked the necessary deep spiritual insight and education and thus found themselves fighting with the papal curia for power, territory, and benefice rather than asserting the actual spiritual authority.

A partial union of the spiritual reign and the ecclesiastic reign in the Czech Lands was already achieved in the 11th century. Premyslid Prince Spytihněv II is believed to have paid the pope one hundred talents of silver so that he would be allowed to wear a bishop mitre during religious holidays even though Prague already had its own bishop. Later on, his brother, the first Czech King Vratislav II, asked the pope for the same privilege. Yet, Charles IV's idea of uniting a spiritual and political authority in one person is not very typical for the Middle Ages and is usually compared with the ruling systems of the ancient Orient or pre-Christian and early Christian Rome. The Emperor — High Priest tried to faithfully fulfill the title he was given: the King and the Emperor of the Holy Roman Empire by the Grace of God. God, if He exists, could not have chosen a better person to fulfill these words than *caesar pontifex maximus Carolus Quartus*, the emperor — bridge builder.

THE FALL OF THE HOLY CITY

Charles Bridge, as one of the most prominent Prague monuments, has also been marked with a later decline and attempts to conceal the real meaning of its legacy. Charles IV's charisma and talent have gone with him. His successors were not capable of carrying on his legacy.

After Charles IV's death on 29 November 1378, his oldest, yet not quite grown-up, son Wenceslas IV automatically assumed the reign. In spite of the fact that Charles IV indulged the young prince with love, care, material things, and a proper education (in occult matters as well), the young inexperienced king did not get much of a chance to continue with the work started by his father. His reign was problem-free only during the first couple of years and became rather shaky already after fifteen years.

During the first decade of Wenceslas IV's rule, the power of the Luxembourgs was still firmly in the hands of the "Prague headquarters." Edifices founded by Charles IV were carried on and new ones were founded. Another esoteric jewel of the city, the Old Town Horologe, which we discussed in a separate book, was being planned and perhaps even constructed during this time.

But Charles IV's original collaborators and political co-creators started leaving this world and their key positions, and the young Wenceslas was not able to adequately replace them. His power was very inconspicuously deteriorating, and it was just a matter of time before someone else would take advantage of the situation.

The "dual throne" was first seriously attacked by the new, young, and ambitious Prague Archbishop Jan of Jenštejn. The Church always resented when religious positions were filled by secular rulers, in particular if they did not at least formally ask for the consent of the Church. And since Wenceslas was not as skillful a politician as his father, Jan of Jenštejn decided to start a new small local war for lay investiture. It was a clash of two irreconcilable fighters. Charles IV's art of compromise, from which he almost always came out as a winner, was forgotten. In the year of 1393, Wenceslas practically lost the war, and it is not really important whether Wenceslas actually disgraced himself with torturing and killing his enemies or whether the crafty Jan of Jenštejn only took advantage of the almost-forgotten modified story about the priest thrown off the Stone Bridge.

Czech historians have been debating for almost two hundred years now whether the cult of Jan of Nepomuk was created just to make people forget Church reformer Jan Hus, burnt at the stake in 1415. In this debate, we can, in good conscience, take the side of Catholic-oriented historians, represented in particular by Josef Pekař, who say that the cult of Jan of Nepomuk would have made its way even if John Hus had not been killed. This petty debate has been carried out vehemently, yet apparently on the wrong battlefield, because this masterful example of falsification of history was to obviously damage the influence and legacy of Wenceslas IV who, as his father, tried to act as emperor — high priest, a secular and ecclesiastic authority independent from Church power.

The result of the war between Wenceslas IV and Jan of Jenštejn was evident. The relationship between Wenceslas IV and the Church was ruined, and the first part of the dual throne collapsed. According to existing documents, Wenceslas fell into a state of apathy and supposedly started drinking, which had devastating effects on the rest of his power. He received a final blow at the break of the century when he was removed from the Roman throne by four electoral votes, which was unprecedented. Wenceslas was unable to protest it and then became a mere puppet in the local power struggle of Czech noblemen and his younger stepbrother Sigismund.

Even though Sigismund of Luxembourg still has a bad reputation in the Czech Lands, it is clear that Sigismund, whom Charles IV made a Hungarian

Wenceslas IV of Luxembourg (1361–1419) was a Czech king and Roman emperor. The son of Emperor Charles VI and his third wife, Anne of Swidnica, was indulged since his childhood with luxury, titles, and the care of the most powerful man of Europe of that time. He received an excellent education, yet never achieved the fame and abilities of his father. In the year of 1400, after twenty-two years of reign, he was removed from the imperial throne. He was also unsuccessful on the national political scene. He was taken hostage by different political groups several times and died on the eve of the Hussite Revolution that subverted almost everything his father had built. His younger brother, Sigismund, took his position on the Czech throne after many years of crusades.

king, was the one who inherited most of his father's talents. But unfortunately not all of them. He made several political mistakes that caused him to never reach the greatness of his father, *sub speciae aeternitatis*. In an attempt to save his brother's collapsing reign in Bohemia for the Luxembourgs, he decided to invade Bohemia and loot its treasure — silver mines in Kutná Hora — which undermined his position in this bearing pillar of Luxembourg imperial power right from the beginning. At the Council of Constance, he succeeded in ending the triple papacy, for which the entire Christian Europe was very grateful to him, and in obtaining a strong position on the imperial throne that he regained for the Luxembourgs. However, the red-haired emperor did not succeed in saving the Czech priest and reformer John Hus from being burnt at the stake. For this reason, he was given the bad nickname "red-haired beast" and lost any chance to become a Czech king.

Due to follow-up unrest, Sigismund decided to move the imperial coronation jewels and the most valuable sacred relics, which had made Prague a real alternative spiritual center of Western Christianity, from Karlstein to Nurnberg. Thus, the city lost most of its magic power. He even took a large part of Wenceslas IV's famous esoteric library from the stronghold by Kunratice. After several lost crusades led by him against Ultraquist Bohemia, Sigismund decided to use his natural political skills, and his political career began to thrive again. In paralyzed Bohemia, he established order and achieved a religious reconciliation, which was rather unusual for that time. And he finally received the so desired Czech crown. But it was too late — he had no time to restore the former splendor and glory of the once shining gem. He died shortly after, without a successor.

The power in the Holy Roman Empire and, several decades later on, in the Lands of the Czech Crown was gradually passed onto the ambitious, yet untalented Habsburg dynasty that consciously resigned on the spiritual dimension of the rule in the Holy Roman Empire and slavishly shared it with the papacy. Gradually, the holiness of the empire vanished and the grace of God from the title "King and Emperor by the Grace of God" withered away; several centuries later, there was nothing left behind the glitter but an empty shell of insignificant pompous titles and positions.

Only once after that, a somewhat enlightened ruler tried to dust off the almost forgotten magic gem in the heart of Europe. It was Habsburg Emperor Rudolph II. He moved his seat to Prague, brought in many excellent scholars of that time (and unfortunately also many crooks), and put together wonderful art collections. However, his attempt to bring out the forgotten potential of the city did not last very long and was met with harsh protests of his own relatives. After his death and a short intermezzo with the Winter King, Frederick of Palatinate, almost everything was destroyed during the Thirty-Year War. Prague was plundered by its spiritual enemies, and art collections and libraries were again looted by foreign armies. Later on, a curtain made of statues of the promoters of the "only true" Christianity dropped on Charles Bridge so that we would not be reminded of the glory and true purpose of this place. For many centuries, the great Czech Kingdom became a province (and a substantial source of wealth) of a neighboring, at one point insignificant, imperial fief.

The statues would probably make a quite pretty sculptural collection on a different bridge for those who prefer form over substance, wouldn't they?

ACKNOWLEDGMENTS

At the end of the book, the author would like to thank all of those who were his light on this journey and without whom it would not have been easy to put some pieces of the puzzle in the right place.

My wife Jarka helped me tremendously with this book. She was my inspiration and the first reader and proofreader of the book. I would like to also thank the artistic jeweler Roman Kotrč from the Charles Bridge Artists Association for the care that the association provides to this monument, as well as for his rings that joined my life not only with my wife but also with this bridge. I thank all those whose books accompanied me on this journey, as well as those who helped to make this publication possible.

When taking the photographs for this book, the photographer, Jan W. Drnek, did not hesitate to risk his own health in the blustering wind and heavy rain.

I gratefully dedicate this book to my eternal friends, the Essene brothers. May this book serve their great honor and glory in the Creation of the Lord since actually two evangelists recorded this remarkable statement of Jesus Christ:

Blessed are the poor in spirit for theirs is the kingdom of heaven... blessed are you when people revile you and persecute you and say all kinds of evil things against you falsely on My account. Be glad and supremely joyful, for your reward in heaven is great, for in this same way people persecuted the prophets who were before you.[10]

Odecha, Adonai!

---

[10] Mt 5,3—12; L 6,20—26

· V ·

EUROPEAN BRIDGES AND ART

BOUQUINISTES

The banks of the Seine River near the Cathedral of Notre Dame have been lined with street sellers of old books and prints, bouquinistes, for centuries. In their green boxes, one can find French classics, valuable prints and old magazine issues.

The word *bouquin*, or *boucquin*, appeared in the French language in the middle of the 16th century, and Savary's Dictionary from 1723 included the word *bouquiniste* for the first time. According to most linguists, it stems from the word boecklin used in Flanders; however, some believe that it originates from the German word Buch or English word book. The first street sellers of books and almanacs emerged in Paris in the 16th century with the boom of book printing.

After Pont Neuf (New Bridge) over the Seine was opened in 1607, several street sellers began selling their books there. In 1620, there were already 24 sellers and they all became a nuisance for bookstore owners who pushed forth a ban on selling books on the street and for some time succeeded.

However, starting in 1670, bouquinistes began selling their merchandise again not only on Pont Neuf but also on the adjacent banks, and after the

Bookstals near the bank of Seine River in Paris, T. F. Simon, 1911.

fall of Bastille and during the time of Napoleon, they spread all the way to Saint Michel Bridge.

Hundreds of people apply for a license every year now, and the waiting period is up to five years. A bouquiniste does not own the box but rents it from the municipal office together with the land and sales right. Every seller may occupy one sales space that does not exceed nine meters of the bank balustrade. All boxes must be painted in green, and no exceptions are tolerated. Nowadays, you can find Paris bouquinistes on eleven banks on both sides of the Seine. Each sells up to 1 500 books, and if they all were open at the same time, readers could choose from 300 000 books.

If you wish to go from Piazza del Duomo to the other side of the Armo River, you must cross Ponte Vecchio, the oldest and most famous bridge in Florence. Its construction started in 1220, it has three vaults and many goldsmith shops built along it. This is why it is also called the Bridge of Goldsmiths.

Nearby is the famous art gallery Galleria degli Uffizi, the largest Italian art collection with real masterpieces; it is one of the most interesting art galleries of the world.

London has a different attraction: the Tower of London with Tower Bridge which, together with Big Ben, is probably the most famous landmark of London. It was finished in 1894, when London was a prominent and flourishing port. The bridge has a sophisticated mechanism that opens the bridge so that large ships could pass through for three minutes.

To make the list of famous European stone bridges complete, we must mention Würzburg and its old principal bridge Alte Mainbrücke. It was built

In Rome, you can see pictures and graphics on the bridge leading to Castel San Angelo. However, it is not as famous as Charles Bridge; Ponte Vecchio is much more famous in Italy.

Stari most

Alte Mainbrücke

jura

Tower Bridge

during the years of 1473 and 1543 to replace a destroyed Roman bridge. During the Late Baroque, it was, similarly to Charles Bridge, adorned with statues of saints; its current look dates approximately from the year of 1730.

And there is also Mostar, Herzegovina, that became famous for its symbol, the old Turkish bridge called *Stari most*. It was built in the 16th century and, with its only vault having a span of almost thirty meters, crosses high above the green waters of the Neretva River and leads into the old bazaar street *Kujundziluk* that connects to the bridge and runs along the left bank, providing beautiful views of the river and city adorned with the verticals of tall slender minarets and mosques, some of which still serve their purpose.

Here, goldsmiths, kujundziluks, sell their gold and silver filigree jewels and other typical Turkish products made of metal, leather and fur. The bridge was destroyed during the Serbian war in the early 1990s and was repaired to its original semblance in 2005.

ON THE PRAGUE BRIDGE

En pragensis ponte,
rescunt sua sponte,
multiflores sine curas
sine ulo fonte.

Every Czech knows the song about how rosemary grows on the Prague Bridge and nobody waters it. Perhaps still in Jan Neruda's lifetime, Charles Bridge knew the bustle of chandlers and herbs-sellers from the Lessor Town and the Old Town.

Charles Bridge became lively again after the tramway and automobile traffic was prohibited there in the 1970s.

The bridge experienced its first surge of artistic excitement during the so-called Prague Spring, when Czechoslovakia searched for its own way of "socialism with a human face." Folk singers and the first artists showed the potential future life on the bridge.

The beginnings of artists selling their work during the "normalization" era were not easy. The police enjoyed charging them with illegal enterprise and many of them even ended up in the prison. The owner of one, historically first official permit from 1984, Jan Procházka, recalls these times:

č.j. 274/84   kopie na vědomí :

Adresa :

Jan Procházka
Sulanského č. 699
Praha 4

Dne 5. 6. 1984 . Výtvarná komise MVP pro dárkové a upomín-
kové předměty se sídlem v Galerii hlavního města Prahy,
Mickiewiczova ul.č.1, Praha 6 - Hradčany posoudila estetic-
kou hodnotu Vámi předložených výrobků :

hlubotiskové reprodukce
        formát 4,5 x 5,5 cm   = 50 ;- Kčs
        formát 6 x 8 cm   = 60,- Kčs
        formát 6 x 18 cm   = 90,- Kčs
        v barevném provedení cena zvýšena o 20,- Kčs

Usnesení :

Výtvarná komise MVP výše jmenované předměty schvaluje
a doporučuje k prodeji.

Toto povolení platí pouze pro prodej v rámci hlavního města
Prahy a Středočeského kraje, pokud žadatelé mají trvalé
bydliště v Praze.
Součástí tohoto povolení je rovněž fotodokumentace výše
uvedených předmětů.

V Praze dne .6. .6. .1984 ...   .
                                       zasloužilý umělec
                                       akad. soch. Štefan Malatinec
                                       předseda Výtvarné komise MVP

....
akad.soch.Dobroslav Kotek
ředitel Galerie hl.m.Prahy

The first official permit to sell artwork during the Communist era.

*When we did not have a permit and we wanted to sell our artwork to tou-
rists, there was always a risk that the police would check us and charge us
with a fine. Sometimes we actually threw our graphics into the river in order
to avoid police chicane. A big turning point came in 1983, when Prague
hosted an international meeting of the youth and the atmosphere became
liberal for a couple of days. A year later, I obtained the first official permit
signed by the director of the Art Gallery of the Capital City of Prague and
the chairman of the Art Commission of the National Committee. It took
another year before I obtained a permit from the District National Committee in Prague 1.*

Roman Kotrč is a native of the Lessor Town. He grew up in Karmelitská Street, and as a child he and his mother Naděžda sold her paintings and his small water-color dogs. Today, he engages in smithcraft; his sign with God's eye adorns the entrance to the art gallery of the Charles Bridge Artists Association located under the bridge on Kampa and is one of the spokesmen of the association.

ARTWORK ON CHARLES BRIDGE

The Charles Bridge Artists Association, a unique civic non-profit association, was founded in 1990. Roman Kotrč, one of its founders and spokesmen, recalls those times:

We founded the association in response to wild capitalism in the early 1990s after the so-called Velvet Revolution. An uncontrolled flood of sellers typical more for a bazaar full of militaria, Russian military hats, cut crystal glass, cheap alcohol, caviar and cigarettes almost drove artists and painters away from the bridge. They tried to draw attention to this situation with a protest strike in 1991 that got huge coverage and started several years of discussion between the association and the Municipal Office for Prague 1. However, similarly to what happened to bouquinistes in Paris, artists were banned from the bridge, but not for long.

As a result of almost three years of discussion, a public call for tenders for sales organization and maintenance of order on Charles Bridge was made in 1993. Winning the call, the association took over the administration of the bridge in the middle of 1993.

During the next years, we started to cooperate with the Art Gallery of the Capital City of Prague in the restoration of statues and statuaries on Charles Bridge, and the cooperation has lasted to this day. The association funded twice the restoration of the statuary of Pieta, the statuary of St. Ivo, the statue of St. Wenceslas, the statue of St. Christopher and the statue of St. Judas Thaddeus and the restoration of the original of the statuary of St. Barbara, St. Margaret and St. Elizabeth made by Ferdinand Max Brokoff. Currently we are funding the restoration of the tenth sculpture on Charles Bridge, the biggest and best-known statuary of St. John of Matha, St. Felix of Valois and St. Ivan, an original made by the same author.

We helped to fund the restoration of the statuary of St. Cyril and St. Methodius, the youngest sculpture on the bridge, that a religious fanatic

Restoration of the statuary of St. John of Matha, St. Felix of Valois and St. Ivan.

damaged with a club in a sudden outburst of madness; luckily, our marshals stopped him before he had a chance to cause more damage. Thanks to the marshals, the repair cost only 3 000 EUR.

Unfortunately, our bridge was not spared of the imported fashion trend, graffiti, that we regularly clean off. Our marshals also try to prevent people from climbing on the statues, which is somewhat Sisyphus work.

The artists, who are on the bridge 365 days a year, make the walk of their fellow citizens and especially tourists on the Royal Way more interesting. Charles Bridge, which is almost seven hundred years old, its statues made throughout three centuries and artists create one of the unforgettable moments in Prague and the Czech Republic.

In addition to its main activity — organizing and maintaining order during the exhibiting and selling of artwork and during public performances on Charles Bridge — the association has some side activities, the goal of which is to help with maintaining and restoring sculptures on the bridge and to inform the public about the association's activity.

The association organizes regular events with young artists who work with association members on Charles Bridge and may join them one day. In order to keep the bridge neat and clean, we had special litter bins made for Charles Bridge.

Nowadays, the association has almost a hundred members, holds a general meeting at least twice a year and organizes a trip by steamboat on the Vltava River for its members and friends once a year in September.

Portraits, paintings, graphics, drawings, photographs, jewelry, designer jewelry, and music – these are techniques and genres that one can see when walking on the bridge. Each year, a special commission evaluates almost a hundred new applications; some of them are really unusual, e.g. pictures painted with chocolate.

Charles Bridge Artists Association o. s.
P. O. Box 106, CZ-118 00 Prague 011
Phone/fax: +420 257 531 088
Address: Sněmovní 7, CZ-118 00 Prague 1
Business hours: Tuesday 9.00 a.m.–12.00 p.m.
                           Thursday 1.00–4.00 p.m.
E-mail: sdruzeni@karluvmost.cz • Http://www.charlesbridge.cz

Each year, 160 artists and 25 musicians present their work on a hundred sales spaces.

In the areas designated for music, you can hear in turn opera singers, jazzmen or glass harmonica players; you can listen to medieval music, an accordion as well as an exotic Australian musical instrument, the didgeridoo.

This sympathetic street-organ player is an Austrian from Vienna. You can also find many other nationalities on Charles Bridge – Russians, Hungarians, Bosnians, Slovaks, Byelorussians, and sometimes even musicians from Brazil.

Association members are very much engaged in the life of the Lessor Town. During the flood in August 2002, they were the first ones to help with the cleaning on Kampa. This photographs are from the February carnival that goes from Pohořelec to Kampa every year. For more information about all events of the association, please visit the website www.charlesbridge.cz.

At night the bridge is totally empty. The artwork is stored in different courtyards and basements of Lessor Town houses.

Charles Bridge during the tragic flood in 1890 that took down several bridge vaults. A temporary foot bridge was used for a long time to cross the Vltava River.

A unique historical picture of the parade of American soldiers on Charles Bridge at the end of May 1945. Throughout the centuries, the bridge has witnessed important events — coronation processions crossed the bridge, the statues looked in silence at the carriage with the dead body of Reinhard Heydrich, the protector of Bohemia and Moravia, during a night ritual procession lit up with torches, American presidents walked on the bridge full of secret agents, Tom Cruise impersonated the main character in the film Mission Impossible here, and the feet of Prague Marathon runners thunder through here every year. (Photo © ČTK)

BIBLIOGRAPHY

- BAIGENT, Michael; LEIGH, Richard; LINCOLN, Henry: Holy Blood, Holy Grail.
- BLÁHOVÁ, Marie et al.: Kroniky doby Karla IV [Chronicles of the Era of Charles IV]. Prague, Svoboda 1987
- BUŘÍVAL, Zdislav et al.: Staletá Praha IX [One-Hundred-Year-Old Prague IX]. Prague, Panorama 1979
- DVOŘÁK, František: Po Karlově mostě [On Charles Bridge]. Prague, NLN 2003
- FULCANELLI: The Mystery of the Cathedrals.
- FULCANELLI: The Dwellings of the Philosophers (I, II).
- GILBERT, Adrian G.: Magi: The Quest for the Secret Tradition.
- HÁJEK of Libočany, Václav: Kronika česká [Czech Chronicle]. Prague, Odeon 1981
- HAVRÁNEK, Edgar Th.: Prsty k obloze — Co vypravují pražské věže [Fingers Pointing to the Sky: What Prague Spires Tell]. Prague, Kuchař 1947
- HEDSEL, Mark, OVASON David: The Zelator
- HERAIN, Jan: Karlův most v Praze [Charles Bridge in Prague]. Prague, Umělecká beseda 1908
- CHADRABA, Rudolf: Staroměstská mostecká věž a triumfální symbolika v umění Karla IV [The Old Town Bridge Tower and Triumphal Symbology in the Art of Charles IV]. Prague, Academia 1971
- CHADRABA, Rudolf: Karlův most [Charles Bridge]. Prague, Odeon, 1974
- KAVKA, František: 5. 4. 1355 — Korunovace Karla IV. císařem Svaté říše římské [5 April 1355: The Coronation of Charles IV as Emperor of the Holy Roman Empire]. Prague, Havran 2002
- KRUŠINA, Zdeněk: Evangelium neznámého eséna [The Gospel of an Unknown Essene]. Prague, Eminent 2005
- KUCHAŘ, Jiří: Esoteric Prague. Prague, Eminent 2002
- LORENC, Vilém: Nové Město pražské [The Prague New Town]. Prague, SNTL 1973
- MALINA, Jakub: The Prague Horologe. Prague, Eminent, 2005
- MEYRINK, Gustav: Neviditelná Praha [Invisible Prague]. Prague, Argo 1993
- MERHOUT, Cyril: Bruncvík na Karlově mostě [Bruncvík on Charles Bridge]. Prague, Společnost přátel starožitností 1941.
- NOVOTNÝ, Kamil, POCHE, Emanuel: Karlův Most [Charles Bridge]. Prague, Pražské nakladatelství V. Poláčka 1947
- New Testament
- OVASON, David: Nostradamus: Is the End of the World Coming?

- PRACNÝ, Petr: Český kalendář světců [The Czech Calendar of the Saints]. Prague, EWA Edition 1994
- RAVENSCROFT, Trevor: The Spear of Destiny
- RAVIK, Slavomír: Velká kniha světců [The Book of the Saints]. Prague, Regia 2002
- SPĚVÁČEK, Jiří: Karel IV. — Život a dílo (1316—1378) [Charles IV: Life and Work Achievements (1316—1378)]. Prague, Svoboda 1979
- STEINER, Rudolf: Theosophy
- STEINER, Rudolf: Egyptian Myths and Mysteries
- STEINER, Rudolf: Learning to See Into the Spiritual World
- STEINER, Rudolf: The Fifth Gospel
- STEINER, Rudolf: The Gospel of St. John
- STEJSKAL, Martin: Praga Hermetica. Prague, Eminent 2003
- STREIT, Jiří: Divy staré Prahy [The Wonders of Old Prague]. Prague, Mladá fronta 1958
- STURLUSON, Snorri: Edda and the Saga of the Ynglings
- SVÁTEK, Josef: Pražské pověsti a legendy [Prague Myths and Legends] (a reprint of the edition from 1883). Prague, Paseka 2002
- SVOBODA, Svatopluk: Praha astrologická [Astrological Prague]. Prague, Melantrich 1994
- ŠPŮREK, Milan: Praga mysteriosa — Tajemství pražského slunovratu [Mysterious Prague: The Secret of the Prague Solstice]. Prague, Eminent 1996
- VANĚČEK, Václav et al.: Karolus Quartus (sborník) [Charles IV (collection)]. Prague, Charles University 1984
- VORAGINE, Jacobi De: The Golden Legend
- ZADROBÍLEK, Vladislav and others a kol.: Opus Magnum (sborník) [Opus Magnum (collection)]. Prague, Trigon 1997

WEBSITES

http://www.catholic-forum.com/saints/
http://pragensia.tiscali.cz/
http://www.feudum.cz/
http://www.wikipedia.org/

ALPHABETICAL INDEX

D

N

O

T

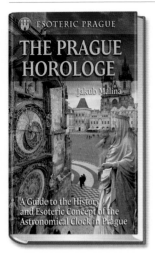

Book describes the history of the building and explains the esoteric symbolism that has survived in the very heart of Prague for six centuries.

In the historical context of the reign of Charles IV, the "last initiated emperor of the Holy Roman Empire," the book talks about the level of occult gnosis of the late Middle Ages and its artistic reflection in architecture, visual arts, and the urbanistic design of the entire city. The book also unfolds the secret of one of the most well-known medieval legends about a blind horologist that has been cited to this day in many other European cities with similar technical machines, e.g. also in Strasbourg, France, or Gdansk, Poland.

Behind the creation of the Prague Horologe, the book discovers the legacy of the Circle and Hammer, one of the first closed esoteric lodges that admitted also lay people and enjoyed the auspices of Roman Emperor Wenceslas IV, son of Charles IV. The interpretation of the symbolism also helps to determine the date of the creation of the building — the documentation of which has disappeared during the centuries — more precisely than official historical literature.

The coronation jewels of the Kingdom of Bohemia are singular and unique. The St. Wenceslas crown is not only a ruler's symbol, but also the symbol of the country. It hides the secret of uniqueness. Its charm lies neither in its antiquity nor in the number of the enchased gems alone. It bears the sanctity and the secret lore assigned to it by Charles IV's commission. Its existence is first mentioned in the protective document from 6 May 1346, issued by Pope Clement VI. After Charles IV's rule, the crown was used for the coronation of twenty-one kings and seventeen queens.

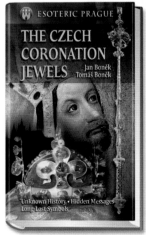

The book The Czech Coronation Jewels is an exceptional addition to the history of the crown, as it — for the first time — offers the possibility to trace the way of thinking of Charles VI, who, when commissioning the making of the crown, contemplated the symbols to be concealed in its form, and the choice and arrangement of its gems.

If we imagine a bird's eye view of Old Prague, there is no question that two colours will dominate: the baked red of the tile roofs and the grey-green verdigris of the cupolas and spires of the cathedrals. We shall encounter these two tinctures, representing the two opposing principles of the alchemical Opus (dry, fiery Sulfur and moist, cold Mercury) in various disguises throughout our journey at every step of the way.

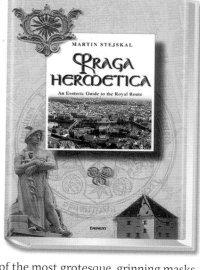

Hence, if we succeed in freeing our sight from Prague's roadways or parterre and lift it upward, we will be surprised by a multitude of thousands of monsters in the form of the most grotesque, grinning masks, looking down contemptuously at our mundane drudgery. Not to mention the old quarters of Prague where one would naturally expect such whirlwind of monsters.

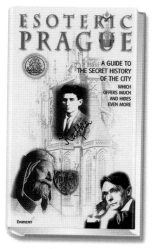

A guide to the secret history of a city which offers much and hides even more. With its hundred spires, its winding cobblestone streets and its secret passageways, Prague remains the magic metropolis of Europe, the city of alchemists and necromancers, a city for those who would like to discover the Truth. Prague observant and full of observers, a city continually experienced and open to everything new issuing from the Light.

FOR MORE INFORMATION VISIT

www.eminent-books.com

ESOTERIC PRAGUE

CHARLES BRIDGE

Jakub Malina

English translation Zuzana Jurgens
Photos Jakub Malina, Jan W. Drnek, Jiří Kuchař, Adam Kuchař
Cover design, layout & typography Adam Friedrich

Printed by Finidr Ltd., Český Těšín

Published by Eminent Publishing House
P. O. Box 298, CZ-111 21 Prague 1, Czech Republic, EU
www.eminent-books.com

07/06/21
ISBN 978-80-7281-305-6